John Steinbeck

John
Steinbeck The Errant Knight

AN INTIMATE BIOGRAPHY OF
HIS CALIFORNIA YEARS

by Nelson Valjean

CHRONICLE BOOKS / SAN FRANCISCO

PHOTOGRAPHIC ILLUSTRATIONS

To
Mary
   the book promised
   so long ago.

To
Dook
   with admiration
   and affection.

AUTHOR'S NOTE

One day in 1930 when I was covering the courthouse for the old *Salinas Index-Journal,* the county treasurer called me to his barred window. "Next time my son's in town," he said, "won't you come over for dinner? He's interested in writing. I think you two would hit it off fine." He paused and stroked his heavy mustache. "Since you're in the newspaper game, maybe you can give him a few pointers."

I laughed at the idea of my giving anyone pointers. "So you want him to win the Nobel Prize?" I chided.

"Oh, he'll win that anyway," the father said.

And, by God, he did!

I never did make that dinner, alas, but I've often thought of my close brush with supreme irony — a newspaper hack giving writing tips to a literary giant in the making. John Steinbeck seems to have done all right on his own.

A week or so after that dinner invitation I was to hear of young Steinbeck again. This was when our society editor told me she had just read his first book, *Cup of Gold,* only recently off the press. "And it wasn't bad."

Her casual remark started me on research that continued for nearly forty years. At first, all I had in mind was a feature for the paper on a budding author from Salinas (he then lived in nearby Pacific Grove), a local-boy-makes-good sort of thing. I was in no hurry. As time scurried by and Steinbeck's output increased, my original idea took broader form. By then I knew the Steinbeck Country as I now know the wrinkles in my face. I had become intimately acquainted with many of his friends from boyhood and high school days, with his parents, relatives, old neighbors, even his detractors. At every opportunity I brought up the subject of Steinbeck, later at home jotting down notes on what I had learned.

And every day between home and the newspaper office, I passed the house in which he was born — a constant reminder not to let go of the literary tiger's tail. Why I hung on, I'm not sure. Pure instinct, I guess. Even when I became managing editor, I still found time for interviews — and not a moment too soon. Some of those interviewees died soon afterward.

How I exulted, I remember, on the day I heard from his high school English teacher who had moved to San Diego. Her lengthy letter detailed classroom recollections of John in his early years and gave her evaluations of his intelligence and mental progress — a rare document indeed.

When I got to know John in Pacific Grove, I told him that some day I wanted to do his biography. A shy person who valued personal privacy above all else, he asked me not to. So I didn't. He was too good a friend to lose. But because of newspaper habits ground into me over the years, I didn't quit researching.

What I wanted to write, if ever so privileged, was a hard-hitting story of the flesh-and-blood Steinbeck. And what a kaleidoscopic life! Tom Sawyer kid days; lover of hills and valleys, rocks and earth, dogs and ponies and people; an off-and-on Stanford student, farmhand, and sugar mill worker. A seaman, road-gang flunkie, hod carrier, and dam builder. A fish hatchery assistant, amateur biologist, avid reader from childhood and — with gusto aplenty — a now-and-then devotee of feminine curves and the bottle. But, most important of all, a gifted, sensitive writer. The book in mind would not be a critical treatise and certainly not hero-worship stuff. Rather, with emphasis on his formative years, it would follow his life in California — his most productive period and, in the opinion of many, the years of his finest work. His move to New York did not alter my sights.

When *East of Eden* was published in 1952 — ten years before the Nobel Prize — I sent him congratulations and laughingly disclosed for the first time his father's remarks in the courthouse so long ago — the far-fetched possibility of my giving him pointers in writing. Also, I told him how sure his father was that one day his son would win the Nobel distinction. He was amused, for, at the time of my note, the Nobel wasn't even a dream. Pure fantasy! His father surely must have been joking. "Being intelligent people," he wrote me, "my parents knew that my chances of making a living at writing were about one in a million — horse racing is a sure thing compared to it." As for the tips in writing, he said, "Believe me, I can still use them." When he did win the Nobel

Prize for Literature in 1962, he was flabbergasted. Later, at his New York home, I couldn't resist saying, "Well, your father was right!" The master of words couldn't find a word to respond.

Since the death of John Steinbeck in 1968, his "personal privacy" no longer matters. And I suspect that he himself would willingly raise the curtain at last while saying, in the vernacular of one of his characters, "Shoot the works!"

ACKNOWLEDGMENTS

My deep appreciation goes to the many people who have lent me papers and photographs or have added their recollections of John Steinbeck to my own. I am especially indebted to Carlton A. Sheffield, the "Dook" of this biography, who cooperated in every way, making available his private documents with no restrictions on their use, letting me read his original early Steinbeck manuscripts and a great batch of Steinbeck letters, and reminiscing deep into the night in his little cabin in Los Altos Hills. We raised many a toast to our mutual friend.

Sincere thanks also go to Elaine Steinbeck and Elizabeth Otis of McIntosh and Otis for permission to use the Steinbeck quotations, to Colonel George Mors, Dr. Frank Fenton, Webster (Toby) Street, Glenn Graves, Lloyd Shebley, Max Wagner, Polly Teas, and Philip J. Planert. The help, encouragement, and pleasant association of Marcia Tucker, who critically reviewed my manuscript, cannot be forgotten.

Further acknowledgments are warmly made to Elizabeth Ainsworth, Robert O. Ballou, Preston Beyer, Leonard Burkat of CBS, Laurence C. Case, *San Francisco Chronicle*, Francis Cislini, Jimmy Costello, Dorothy Covici, R. B. Cozzens, Bernice Donahue, Dorothy Donahue, Ted Durien, Mr. and Mrs. Harold R. Ebright, Jr., Horace R. (Sparky) Enea, *San Francisco Examiner*, Joseph Fontenrose, Nan Fowler, Dell Gard, Mrs. Ben Graves, Harvey Hall (registrar of Stanford University), Mildred Hargis, Lena Hayes, Pauline Holm, Charlotte Jackson, Frank B. Jacobson, (principal, Montery High School), L. E. (Eddie) Johnson, Lawrence William Jones, Helen Leavitt, Goddard Lieberson (president, CBS), and Dr. Harry R. Lusignan.

J. Wilson McKenney, Emmett G. McMenamin, Ralph Moreno, *San Francisco News*, Thelma Percy, Mrs. Robert Petersen, Helen Reed, Rose Rhyner, Edward Ricketts, Jr., Esther Rodgers, Susan R. Rosenberg (assistant archivist, Stanford University Libraries), Leo

Shapovalov (senior fish biologist, California Fish and Game Department), John D. Short, Jr., Edward Silliman, Mrs. Roth Speakman, Elinor B. (Jeri) Spowers, William Stephens, Virginia Unsworth, Dorothy Vera, Henry Meade Williams, and Norabelle Wright.

And finally thanks are due the helpful researchers in the Mill Valley Public Library, Monterey Library, New York Public Library, San Francisco Public Library, Stanford University Libraries, and the John Steinbeck Public Library in Salinas.

PROLOGUE

An undercurrent of hostility ran through the handsome living room. Every so often its sweep reached the small clusters of guests standing about and even nudged the hostess, who was doing her best to remain calm and smiling as skipper of the buffet table. Almost everyone had a glass in hand. It was a warm summer evening in Salinas, California, early in the 1970s.

As a former resident back on a brief visit, I had been invited that very afternoon to this informal party hosted by one of the town's more solid citizens. Only a few there knew me, and I preferred it that way.

The company was fairly representative, consisting of Main Street businessmen, a few retired old-timers, lettuce nabobs, clubwomen, and assorted others. Typically, most of the conversation touched on personalities, crop acreage, local events. Once in a while, though, that disquieting undercurrent surfaced, eliciting scowls and an occasional raised voice. It was puzzling until I caught the name of Steinbeck, pronounced with unmistakable bitterness. Then I began to understand, for to many of the older inhabitants of Salinas, John Steinbeck was a betrayer of his birthplace, a maligner of decent people — honest farmers and shippers — and dirty-minded as well. Those things could not be forgotten, even after more than thirty years. Many of them feared that some of the books he had written had planted seeds for future labor unrest in their fertile valley.

"Mr. Too-Big-for-His-Britches" was dead now, but the anger remained. It didn't matter that he had left the region as a young man, eventually to win the Nobel Prize for Literature, or that he came from an old and respected family. Whenever the conversation turned to agriculture, as conversations usually did sooner or later, his name crept in, bringing irritation and often hatred with it.

Beside the portable bar stood a balding man whose florid face ran wet from the effects of alcohol and indignation. Downing a shot of bourbon, he turned to a fellow drinker and snorted over the humming voices: "We shoulda lynched the son of a bitch to begin with!" A warning touch from his wife went unheeded. "Bastard nearly ruined this town. . . ." His listener, attempting to defend the novelist, was stared down.

Two elderly women sat with a younger one chatting idly, toying with their plates of food. Their conversation drifted to the Wanderers' Club — once a very proper, top-drawer women's organization in town. Soon one of the oldsters began digging into its past. And up popped the devil again — by name, John Steinbeck! Sitting at the far end of the divan, I stirred. Right after one of his first books was published, the speaker recalled, Olive Steinbeck, John's mother, had her son autograph some copies and brought them to a Wanderers' meeting, proud as could be. She wanted her fellow club members to have them, with her compliments. But what books they were — "lust, sex, vile words!" Naturally the gifts were refused, flat-out turned down. So Olive had to pack that "trash" right back home.

The speaker's story at that point obviously distressed the younger woman, who complained of feeling ill and left. The tale-bearer blamed the potato salad and put aside her own plate.

Next morning I spent some time exploring the town, which was a "town" no longer but a city of 60,000. As I stood admiring the beautiful downtown library, my guide, an old friend, brought up a revealing incident. When the library directors had considered naming the building after the novelist, a clergyman on the board objected. An investigation had shown him, he said, that the writer's personal life would not set a very good example for boys and girls coming in for books — "Steinbeck roamed quite a bit." But the reverend lost out. His protests were overridden, and the impressive building officially became the "John Steinbeck Public Library."

In a letter to me some time before all this, Steinbeck had written: "It occurs to me that probably the most heartbreaking title in the world is Tom Wolfe's *You Can't Go Home Again* — it's literally true. They want no part of me [in Salinas] except in a pine box."

Although one Salinas faction finds it hard to forget old animosities, another and vastly larger group has a deep appreciation of his work. They are proud, too, that the writer's old home is in their town. Some years ago, the first public interest was shown in the dwelling, which was then privately owned. Maintenance and repairs were a costly problem.

14

Ownership changed hands several times. Then along came the Valley Guild, an energetic, non-profit, highly regarded organization, with an idea. Anxious to assure that the writer's birthplace and boyhood home would be saved as a literary shrine — and pay its own way while doing so — the guild purchased the property and transformed it into a gourmet eating place, with all profits going to selected Salinas Valley charities. It's the kind of project John Steinbeck himself would have approved of.

A hundred years from now, his followers agree, the works of John Steinbeck will still be making people laugh and cry and think.

He just won't stay in a pine box.

CHAPTER ONE

ΑT about two o'clock in the afternoon on February 27, 1902, Norris & Rowe's Big Trained Animal Show was getting underway in the growing hamlet of Salinas, California. Farmer folk from miles around were there, as were red-headed Esther Steinbeck, almost ten, and her sister, Beth, a blonde of seven.

Sitting in the crowded grandstand, they soaked up every precious moment and applauded often, from the opening appearance of the camels, elephants, zebras, ponies, and goats to the introduction of the No-Such-Animal, an anteater, which they agreed was the most comical-looking creature they'd ever seen. And, of course, they howled over the antics of the "twenty funny clowns." Time after time they reminded themselves to thank their father, who back home had so generously pressed upon them the price of tickets and crackerjack and almost eagerly sent them out of the house and on their way.

When at last the show was over, the sisters left the tent and headed home, two blocks away. Reaching the ornate, mid-Victorian dwelling at 130 Central Avenue (since renumbered 132), they pushed through the gate and hurried up the veranda steps. Their beaming father stood at the door and softly announced that here, during their absence, had been the day's real Main Event. Their mother had brought them a surprise — a baby brother! Good Dr. Murphy had already come and gone.

A brother, how wonderful! A baby brother! And all the while, they had half-expected another sister. Instantly all circus visions dissolved under the greater interest. Scarcely breathing, the girls tiptoed inside to get their first look at the brand-new man in the house. Although they were much too young to think of his future then, their mother had. Already she was hoping he'd become a banker or at least an accountant, something sound and practical.

The many-gabled house provided a propitious debut for John Ernst Steinbeck — a vast setting of high ceilings, shafts of sunlight, mysterious attic rooms, nooks and shadows that demanded exploration, a front door whose inset of stained glass shimmered with color, and a cellar stocked with preserves. John would one day put that cellar to still further use, turning it into his "opium den" and dungeon for prisoners of war.

In his earliest years the house was his whole world, although he was seldom permitted into the front parlor, which was kept darkened, dustless, and closed off with sliding doors. A sitting room was the family gathering place. The dining room, with its big table and precisely arranged glass and china cupboards, held promise, as did the kitchen, spice-scented on cookie-baking days. There was also a guest room on the main floor. His mother, Olive — short, comely, with a button nose — bustled about the house constantly. Her high-busted figure resembled a pouter pigeon's.

Of all the rooms, John probably liked the general sitting room best of all. It was comfortable and informal, and it was here after dinner that his mother and father took turns reading aloud from the popular and classical literature which filled the house. From the *Alice* books to *Treasure Island*, the lively tales held them all spellbound. Scripture was also read. If his parents were too busy for the story hour, the child would pore over words and pictures himself, having learned to read when exceptionally young; it was a momentous day when, at age four, he discovered that certain simple words rhymed.

One of John's early memories was of the earthquake that sawed along the San Andreas Fault in 1906, wiping out much of San Francisco and tattering Salinas. Taken by his father down Main Street after the quake, the four-year-old boy looked upon tons of scattered brick and broken glass and a whole streetful of rubble from the fallen Ford & Sanborn Mercantile Store. Although his own home escaped major damage, the chimney had behaved most peculiarly, twisting completely around. The boy's worst pang was over the family's first phonograph, which crashed so hard it never spoke again.

Surrounded by a picket fence, the story-and-a-half Steinbeck dwelling distinctly spelled upper middle class and respectability in that sprawling town of 3,000. The neat lawn and flowers were the admiration of the neighborhood. A man named J. J. Conner had built the wonderful house before the 1900s, and while he was never to live in it, he took pride in its stone and scantling, scrollwork and gingerbread.

In John's childhood, no one would have guessed his future, not even from his book hunger and fascination with words, which wasn't thought unusual for the son of an ex-schoolmarm. He was tall and heavy-boned for his age, with wavy dark brown hair, a high wide forehead, prominent nose, and full lips. One arresting feature was a peculiar blueness of eye, a haunting, almost luminous shade. At parties he would sit apart, silent and moody, a trait which sometimes caused him to be labeled "stuck up." A tight, high-strung bundle of contradictions, spoiled, headstrong, and restless, John, when not withdrawn, could be an almost overbearing showoff. He was always unpredictable. Certainly he did not fit the standard human mold.

"I remember the sorrow at not being a part of things in my childhood," he says in *Journal of a Novel*. And, "Something cuts me off always." In lessening degree his shyness persisted throughout life. On the other hand, when willing and anxious to play, he usually insisted on being "head man." Glenn Graves, a neighborhood chum, received a toy train one Christmas. John was invited to help make it go but wouldn't touch it unless he could be engineer. For once he was refused — and never did play with Glenn's exciting toy.

At another time, Glenn said to his mother, "When I grow up, I'm going to be vice-president of the United States."

"But why don't you want to be president?" his mother asked.

"Oh, *John's* going to be president," Glenn answered.

A broad streak of Tom Sawyer ran through young Steinbeck's makeup, a strange quality for one so shy. John was a born mischief-hunter, mischief-maker, and lover of derring-do. In future stories he often called upon incidents and emotions from his boyhood.

On an upended crate in the Graves's barn a lantern glowed. Its light faintly outlined the family horse nodding in a corner, glinted upon garden tools, and shimmered over the polished spokes of a stored carriage. Ranged in a semi-circle in front of the lantern were bags of grain, and on each bag sat one or more neighborhood youngsters. They listened spellbound to the boy in knee pants standing before them, the crate serving as his lectern, the dim lantern as his floodlight. In hushed tones he reviewed their reason for meeting. They must deal at once with the Yellow Peril. It was getting worse all the time. The Japs would be invading America any day now. The papers said so.

John paused, glowered into the barn's dark reaches, and turned the lantern down still more. He was mighty thankful, he whispered fiercely, that he'd organized the B.A.S.S.F.E.A.J. when he did. No time to lose. Members of the Boys' Auxiliary Secret Service for Espionage Against the Japanese must wear disguises at all times and spy in absolute silence, he cautioned. At that moment one boy sneezed. John shushed him instantly, repeating the need for secrecy — "And don't tell anybody our meeting place! Not even your mothers!" He instructed his eager agents to raise their right hands and repeat after him: "I am ready to die for my country when my country calls." When this solemn vow was taken, he waved several sheets of writing paper, the society's constitution and by-laws, which were so important he had drawn them up himself in his attic bedroom. After reading them aloud, he bowed humbly, promising to give his all as the society's president, a post to which he had appointed himself that very morning.

It would be the duty of fellow spies, he went on dramatically, to find the home of every Japanese living in the Salinas Valley and mark its location with a cross on a map he'd bring. Patiently he assigned his listeners to undercover work in various Salinas neighborhoods — valley appointments would come later. This delicate procedure went smoothly until the smallest member, Billie Smeed, started crying because his spying would be limited to the grounds of the Catholic church. But John softened the blow by saying, "Some day when there's war, we'll turn over our map to the gover'ment — and be heroes."

Signaling for strict attention, he made a chilling announcement. Each member must sign the constitution in blood! While shudders swept the group, he produced a pin for bloodletting and a pen, but finally yielded to protests and accepted mere droplets of crimson. The rolled-up documents, inserted in a can, were being hidden over a rafter when Glenn Graves's all-knowing mother called from her kitchen door: "Come out of the barn, children. Come get your cookies and milk."

The boys flung open the barn doors and scrambled outside, John tagging along behind. On the way to the kitchen he was heard to grumble, "Cookies and milk! Christ a'mighty!"

The episode of the bold spying society appeared in *The Pastures of Heaven*, published in 1932. Basic facts were retained, though the barn meeting went unmentioned. But what became of the B.A.S.S.F.A.J.? More than fifty years later in his New York apartment John gave the answer. Gazing from a window overlooking the city's great skyline, he mused, "I remember our boyhood chagrin when Takashi Kato heard of our society and begged to join it. He was a Japanese-American and our best friend. We had to tell him we were spying on the Japs and couldn't accept him. He was near tears. The poor kid blinked and mumbled, 'Well, I want to join anyway. We can mark on the map where my father lives.' After that, there was nothing to do but disband. And we did. It was a lasting lesson in racial friendship."

In the Graves household on the morning after the barn meeting, breakfast was a quiet affair. When Mr. Graves had eaten and departed for his ranch, Mrs. Graves waited for her son's usual chatter. But his lips were sealed, his mind no doubt filled with his new responsibilities and the need for a disguise. From time to time his head jerked a little and his shoulders twitched. His mother studied him. Looked closer still. Then she pounced — and plucked from his neck a grayish speck. Gingerly she peeked at it between her thumb and forefinger. It moved. And on that infinitesimal note the day's trouble began.

Instantly, on sighting the louse, Mrs. Graves knew its source. A few nights before, two tramps had been given permission to sleep in the barn. They must have left vermin, just lying in wait for tender new fields. As distasteful as it was, she folded the evidence in toilet paper, ordered her son not to move until her return, and grimly marched across the street to the Steinbeck home.

Olive answered the doorbell, expressing surprise over her early caller, and led the way into the sitting room. The two women settled into facing chairs, Mrs. Steinbeck keeping her eyes on the mysterious packet. But Mrs. Graves was in no hurry to end the drama. It wasn't until she had sketched background details that she unfolded her tissue-wrapped bombshell.

If Mrs. Graves had been upset, Olive was thunderstruck. Why, her own son must be — God forgive the word! — *buggy*. Mrs. Graves stood up and made ready to leave. She had other calls to make. As she left she was clutching her neatly refolded square of toilet paper.

Home at noon, Mr. Steinbeck treated the problem lightly. But just the same, he did as directed, drawing a tub of hot water and going to work on his offspring with a bar of yellow soap, smarting disinfectants, washcloths, and a scrubbing brush. Throughout the hot, harsh treatment, John kept yowling through the steam, "But I *want* lice!"

The boy never forgot the morning of the burning bath. All next day, riding his bicycle was painful. This was a handicap, for he needed his bike on his *Morning Journal* route, a job on which he brazenly made his own rules — prophetic of another newspaper job at another time, 3,000 miles away. Throwing papers wasn't much fun; he vastly preferred watching ants at work or robins building a nest, which proved costly indeed. For each subscriber missed, he was fined ten cents, publisher

Paul Parker explaining that the fines would teach the boy to remember. John called him Simon Legree to his face. When overlooked subscribers phoned their complaints to the *Journal* and their messages were relayed to 130 Central, the senior Steinbeck himself would often deliver the forgotten papers fast and inconspicuously.

As John pedaled up Archer Street on his newspaper route, his hound Gulliver barking at his side, he spotted elderly Miss Rankin waiting in her yard. She looked unhappy about something as she came to the curb to accept her *Journal*, and John fully expected a bawling out; God knows, he had missed her house often enough. Instead, sniffling a little, Miss Rankin explained that her little dog, Trixie, had been gone for two days now. If John could find Trixie, she would reward him with a silver dollar. He promised to search. As he rode away, Gulliver following, Miss Rankin was opening the paper to "Pets Lost and Found."

By the end of the week he had almost forgotten the incident when another customer stopped him to tell of the disappearance of still another dog. No reward was offered, however, and he was unimpressed.

On carrier payday the entire matter had left his mind. He had gone through an entire two weeks without missing a subscriber! Publisher Parker congratulated him, observing that the fines were apparently turning him into a good businessman.

Already John knew how he'd spend his pay, or part of it. Without telling his parents, he led his little sister Mary — three years his junior — to the faded green house of Ramon Rodriquez some blocks away. Mrs. Rodriguez made and sold tamales, tortillas, and other Mexican dishes, most of which went into private homes.

Mary was thrilled. This was her first visit, although John had been there often and once had brought home some tamales, which his mother promptly threw out. Possessing all the sociability of *Tortilla Flat's* Señora Cortez, fat, aproned Mrs. Rodriguez greeted John warmly and made much of his sister. Her floured hands and arms shooed away her own brood of six. When John explained that he and Mary wanted to buy a tamale apiece and eat them there, Mrs. Rodriguez asked if they had their mother's permission. John avoided an answer by also ordering some frijoles. Their pleased hostess waddled into her factory-kitchen and seated her young guests at an oilcloth covered table in the corner, while her own youngsters, giggling, peeked 'round the door.

The tasty tamales were big and the beans steaming hot. When Mrs. Rodriguez asked if the children wanted milk, John, eying a bottle of beer on the drainboard, hinted at a different preference. Mrs. Rodriguez obliged, pouring small quantities of the brew into two glasses with the comment that it couldn't hurt them. John slipped a tortilla tidbit into his pocket for Gulliver.

For a half hour Mary and John gorged themselves, eating until they could eat no more, their faces streaked with tamale sauce and bean juice. Talkative from the effects of the beer, John disclosed that he had had his biggest payday yet and that he'd have earned still more money if he had found Miss Rankin's dog — a black and white bitch worth a reward of a whole dollar.

"*Madre de Dios*'" exclaimed Mrs. Rodriguez. "I think I saw that *perra* in my own yard! But I guess she run away some place with a husban'. She is not in the yard now. Poor Miss Rankin." She paused, clucking her tongue. 'Ai, an' worth a whole dollar!'"

Out on the street, the bill paid, brother and sister, with the help of a little spittle, scoured the telltale signs from each other's face and headed home — for dinner.

Some years later when John learned that the Board of Health had cracked down on Mrs. Rodriguez for using dogs in her genuine beef tamales, his eyes flickered but not for gastronomic reasons. He felt sorry for Miss Rankin and little Trixie, he said, but indignantly demanded to know why Mrs. Rodriguez hadn't boiled up some of the cats in town instead of "man's best friend!"

CHAPTER TWO

THERE was no majestic Mississippi River flowing grandly by for the Salinas Tom Sawyer, but there were sloughs. In the old days they had been invaluable in helping to drain a region once marshland — a country top-layered with rich silt deposited through the ages by the periodically overflowing Salinas River, and where almost anything would grow. The sloughs ran sluggishly through the town in the wet season, twisting this way and that, looping around, and downtown they were crossed by footbridges or sturdy walks. And most were narrow enough for a boy to jump across. In some places they left little tule-filled ponds where frogs bellowed and a kid could get a jar of pollywogs to hide under his desk at the West End School. ("It is possible that if in the night the frog sound stopped, everyone in Salinas would have awakened, feeling there was a great noise." — *East of Eden.*)

But the principal racket in those days came from the chugging autos which were increasingly competing with horse-drawn vehicles, even though the Dashaway Stables on Main Street were still doing a lively business. The rattling and honking was heard both on out-of-town lanes and in the four blocks comprising the business district, from one end of "hard" Main Street to Castroville Street and out to where it angled west, through sugar beet and potato lands and fields of wild mustard, to the country crossroads of Castroville, nine miles away. John liked horses but he liked tin lizzies, too.

When autos frightened horseflesh, the town almost sighed in relief. Salinas needed stirring up. It was a drowsy town, just beginning to come awake. One day P. Tagglio, a hog buyer, pulled his team and light buggy in front of Griffin Bros. Meat Market. When he alighted, the team took off. Frank Griffin, the market owner, jumped on a nearby nag and galloped after the runaways. As the team passed the Salinas Hotel on West Market Street, the pursuer hurtled into the buggy seat. When he drove the team back down Main, more than a mile from the starting point, he was hailed as a hero. John heard the story many times and retold it to his playmates. Griffin was his good friend.

One thing the inquisitive boy didn't tell was of his occasional explorations of Chinatown on the upper end of Soledad Street, across the railroad tracks. Here the street was lined with squat, ramshackle structures, and John could hear gambling inside — the singsong of fantan dealers, click of chips, rattle of dominoes, and clink of silver dollars. Exciting sounds. He tried to act unconcerned when Chinese men shuffled past on the sidewalk. And once he caught a glimpse of Shorty Lee, tong leader and unofficial "mayor" of Chinatown, and Ah Tye, leader of an opposing tong. The two enemies were only a few feet apart. The boy, anticipating bloodshed, ducked into a black and pungent alley. He could hear a shrill exchange of words — but, disappointingly, nothing happened. ("And do you remember how an easterly breeze brought odors from Chinatown, roasting pork and punk and black tobacco smoke and yen shi?" — *East of Eden.*) Once he peeked into forbidden California Street where The Row began, a block from Chinatown. Blinds were drawn. When he heard of a lady named Fartin' Jenny, he thought it wicked indeed. This was something to whisper about to playmates. The name must have made an impression, for he used it in a later story, and, of course, "the spangled palaces of sin" played a major role in *East of Eden*. His descriptions were borrowed from boyhood recollections, even to the tall grass that bordered the street opposite the bordellos in the spring — with "wild oats and mallow weeds and yellow mustard mixed in." Also remembered were the freight trains thundering past on the nearby Southern Pacific tracks, their blinding headlights knifing the darkness.

The West End School was not far from his home, as was Baby School, which he attended through the first and second grades. The Episcopal church was inescapable. Dressed in his Sabbath best, shoes blackened, he would try vainly to slick down his curly hair before setting out for Sunday school with neatly dressed Mary, who would try on this one day not to be a tomboy. In their ears would be a ringing warning from their parents to mind their manners in church, which they did, mostly.

On his bike in late spring he would explore the countryside, pedaling out to dried-up Heinz and Mud "Lakes," finding fields of barley to hide in, creeping up on nests of meadowlarks, looking over vast fields of beets destined for the Spreckels beet sugar factory, and watching wild pigeons in the sky. ("A flight of birds rolled and twisted high overhead, and they caught the last light on their flickering wings, and twinkled like little stars." — *To a God Unknown.*)

And sometimes without telling his parents he rode to one or another of three swimming holes in the Salinas River four miles away, where he would meet John Murphy, son of the doctor who delivered him, Eddie Johnson, and other friends near his own age. All were good swimmers, John Steinbeck one of the best. At such times his shyness wasn't apparent. One swimming hole which they seldom used was near the Salinas River bridge at Davis Crossing; their favorite was the Boy Scout hole, popular with the Scouts later in the season. It had jetties from which to dive and there were not many overhanging willows. Sometimes they swam in the impounded waters above Toro Creek dam, but the waters were often muddy and at some points the banks held a jelly of quicksand.

Hankering for a swim one sultry day in early summer and lacking time for the river, he headed on his bike for a familiar ranch on the old Blanco Road, two miles from his home, which was owned by Ben Graves, father of Glenn, who went there daily from his own home on Central. Presently the operational center of Graves's sixty acres of beans and sugar beets slid into view — a spread of barn, bunkhouse, windmill, and water tower.

When John reached the base of the water tower, he looked around cautiously. No one in sight. Skinning out of his clothes, he climbed the tower ladder rapidly and soon stood on the narrow platform near its top, stark naked. Much of Salinas and the surrounding country lay sprawled below.

How dinky the town was! How cramped and dinky! And he'd always pictured it as a vast city. It may have crossed his mind to wonder if he'd grow up to be a farmer like his grandfather, and almost everybody else he knew. While he loved the soil and everything that grew, he didn't want to farm. Peering over the tank's rim, where there was an opening in its roof, his sense of excitement rushed back. The cistern was more than half full. A ladder attached to the wall inside the wooden tank led down below the surface, but he ignored this troublesome way of descent. His supple, long-legged body went arcing outward and down.

The mammoth vat made a fine deep swimming pool — better than the river. Here a boy could splash around to his heart's content, without risk of collision; submerge without thought of tangling underbrush; float and look upward at the weather roof where light feebly filtered through, and not get snagged by willows. Disadvantages were few — the worst, the gloom and the silence. Sounds were swallowed up within the vast circular wall of his private pool. Just what would have happened in the event of a sudden cramp or other mishap, there's no telling. However, he himself has said that no thought of danger crossed his mind. Finally tiring, he grabbed a slippery lower rung and, dripping, pulled himself upward. At the top, on the sun-drenched platform, he rested a few minutes before starting down the outside ladder. Someone shouted. Mr. Graves was coming on the run.

"Hey, you, John Steinbeck!" the ranch owner yelled. "Get down! Get right down! Damn kids!" He launched into a tirade and sputtered about the ever-present danger.

John dropped to the ground and reached for a grain bag to finish drying. Even at that age, he neither flinched nor backed down in the face of a critic.

By this time Mr. Graves had worked himself into a red-faced fury. "Besides, my hired hands *drink* this water," he fumed. "We want to keep it clean, y'hear?" It was John's turn to lose his temper. "I'm not dirty!" he cried, drawing himself up, arms akimbo on naked hips. "Anyway, ain't your tank outlet screened?

Mr. Graves was so taken aback with this strange reasoning that all he could do was stand and gape. Later, though, he recounted the incident many times, always generously allowing that John may have had a point, after all — maybe the outlet strainer *would* have trapped at least the big microbes.

CHAPTER THREE

"THIS solitary peak [Fremont's Peak] overlooks the whole of my childhood and youth, the great Salinas Valley stretching south for nearly a hundred miles, the town of Salinas where I was born now spreading like crab grass toward the foothills. . . . I felt and heard the wind blow up from the long valley. It smelled of the brown hills of wild oats." — *Travels with Charley*.

Alisal Park was ideal for picnics. To reach the oak-shaded grounds six miles east of Salinas, families traveled by horse and buggy or took the adventuresome "P. V." — the narrow-gauge Pajaro Valley Consolidated Railroad. The little engine, belching black smoke, pulled its string of crowded, swaying little cars from Salinas out to Spreckels and then doubled back cross country. The children aboard screamed in delight, courting couples held hands, and the older folks watched the beet fields flying past at twenty miles an hour.

The picnic area was especially popular in late spring and summer. Tucked in a fold of the lower Gabilans, it had numerous picnic tables and ample room for dancing. On special occasions a civic group would sponsor an outing, and the Salinas City Band would tootle throughout the day. Joe Connors, primed with beer, would warble a few Irish ballads and crowds would line up at the charity booths. You could eat a bellyful, too. Sizzling steaks moved endlessly from the grills. Lemonade was gulped by the gallon. And great wedges of cake, brought by the church ladies, were devoured. Over this whole lively scene, the smell of burning oak vied with the fleeting scent of wildflowers.

The Steinbecks preferred quieter picnics as a rule but sometimes attended the noisy ones. While John lost some of his usual reserve at the big affairs, and even cheered a little at the portable shooting gallery, he could usually be seen talking with his younger sister or trudging along the ferny banks of Alisal Creek. At one of the busier outings Mrs. Graves came up and asked over the noise of the merrymaking if he were having a good time. His noncommittal answer: "I guess so." Clearly, the only times he ever really let loose were on the streets of his own neighborhood.

As a boy, John may or may not have visited the ranch of his immediate antecedents in southern Monterey County. Although in *East of Eden* he appears on intimate terms with that ranch, neither of his older sisters believes he went there in his youth. Alisal Park near the Old Stage Road was barely on the fringe of the country his pen would immortalize. It was an important fringe, though, and probably marked his deepest penetration to date of the "long valley."

Of his twenty-eight books a dozen are set between the Pacific Ocean and the rugged Sierra Nevada Mountains, north of Los Angeles and south of San Francisco — an area encompassing both the Monterey Peninsula on the coast and the Salinas Valley about thirty miles inland but paralleling the sea. The long valley extends for a hundred miles, finally emptying its river — the Salinas — through a break in the coastal range into Monterey Bay.

When John finally did go south, he passed through the hot sleepy hamlets of Chualar, Gonzales, Soledad, and Greenfield before reaching King City, the community of his forebears, some sixty miles below his hometown. Sometimes the willow-shaded Salinas River was within sight of both the highway and rail line; never was it far away. To the east of the valley rose the Gabilan Mountains, crested with pine and often broken with fingers of rock, its lower slopes dotted with farms. In *East of Eden* the Gabilans were ". . . full of sun and loveliness and a kind of invitation . . .," while he saw the Santa Lucia range to the west as ". . . dark and brooding — unfriendly and dangerous," its sequoia forests a trap for ocean fogs. So closely is the entire region identified with the author that it is often referred to, simply, as Steinbeck Country.

Here was country that, through the checkers of chance, brought together interesting traits from his German-Irish ancestors. Did he inherit, in some measure, both his sense of practicality and his vivid imagination? And what of his strange and contradictory nature? Like John, his forebears were peripatetic.

Some fifty years before John's birth, a young Massachusetts woman named Almira Ann Dickson took a trip to Jerusalem, accompanied by her parents and sisters. While in the Holy Land she met John Adolph Grosssteinbeck (the original Steinbeck family name was spelled with three *s*'s), a German visitor from Elberfeld (Wuppertal), about twenty miles south of Dortmund. He was seventeen and a cabinetmaker. The two fell in love and were married in the Holy Land on June 1, 1856, as were another Dickson sister and another Grosssteinbeck on this romantic journey. Within a few years John Adolph and his wife came to the United States, finally settling in St. Augustine, Florida, where he resumed work in cabinet shops and his wife gave birth to author John's father, the first John Ernst Steinbeck. After, serving in the Civil War with the Confederate Army, into which he was drafted, John Adolph moved with his family to Leominister, Massachusetts. Several years later California beckoned. Traveling overland to the Golden State, he opened a flour mill in Hollister in 1874. Later that same year, on November 11, his family left Leominister to rejoin him just in time for Thanksgiving. Within two years the family was in comfortable circumstances. They bought ten acres near Hollister and planted fruit trees, at the same time gaining a wide reputation for hard work and honesty.

In 1890 their son John Ernst, the third of five sons, moved to King City, Monterey County. There he was much taken with the charm, erudition, and plain spunk of Olive Hamilton, a schoolteacher, who had begun her teaching career at seventeen. She had taught in one-room schoolhouses in Monterey County — in Peachtree on the Mustang Grade, Pleyto, and the remote and rugged Big Sur, reachable only on horseback. An incident from their romance appears in *Travels with Charley:* "And on one of those oaks my father burned his name with a hot iron together with the name of the girl he loved." Olive and John were married. They were living in King City when their first child, Esther, was born on April 14, 1892.

An 1892 Great Register of Monterey County, compiled for voting purposes, provides a clue to the appearance of Steinbeck's father: "John Ernst Steinbeck, 29, six feet tall, fair complexion, blue eyes, brown hair, scar on left cheek, a native of Florida and a bookkeeper in King City." In general, he looked somewhat like his future son, the author John Steinbeck, would look when he was twenty-nine.

Irish blood flowed strong in Olive's veins. Her father, Samuel Hamilton, was the son of small country farmers in Mulkeraugh, less than twenty miles northeast of Londonderry, a man of "good looks and charm and gaiety." In 1851 he broke tradition, leaving the stone house where his ancestors had lived for hundreds of years, and rounded the Horn on his way to California; his wife Elizabeth (Liza), also from Northern Ireland, came by way of the Isthmus of Panama. Although their early movements on the West Coast are uncertain, near the end of the Civil War they were living in San Jose where Olive was born on December

11, 1866. Subsequently, Samuel homesteaded a ranch east of King City in Monterey County, which his grandson was to write about so movingly in *East of Eden*. Also a blacksmith and well-borer, Samuel invented and improved many farm instruments for himself and his Salinas Valley neighbors. If one were to search for literary signposts in John Steinbeck's forebears, it would have to be Samuel, with his great "gift of blarney." ("It was a very bad day when three or four men were not standing around the forge, listening to Samuel's hammer and his talk." — *East of Eden*.)

For a time Olive, her handsome new husband, and the baby continued to make their home in the hot, dry community of King City. They next moved to Paso Robles, where John Ernst worked for the Southern Pacific flour mill. Following the birth there of a second child, Elizabeth (Beth), on May 25, 1894, they settled permanently in Salinas. At first John Ernst worked for the Sperry Flour Company, becoming manager, then operated his own hay, grain, and feed store on Main Street, did a stint for the Spreckels Beet Sugar Company, and served for eleven years as county treasurer. His wife became an active clubwoman and with boundless energy organized various drives and movements. Their only son was born on February 27, 1902. A little less than three years later, on January 9, 1905, their last child, a daughter Mary, arrived. Close bonds of affection marked the relationship of Mary and her brother.

Like his grandfather Samuel, John had a passion for inventing things, as he stressed time and again in *Journal of a Novel*. ". . . inventions and designs are the same as writing. I come from a long line of inventors. This is in my blood. We are improvisors. . . ." He loved tools of just about every kind. When touring the country in preparation for *Travels with Charley*, in Monterey he looked up an old friend, Webster (Toby) Street. Together they called at Holman's Department Store in Pacific Grove and visited the tool department. John admired a spokeshave — a blade with a handle at either end used to fashion wagon spokes, a rarity these days — and urged Toby to buy it. "What on earth for?" Toby asked. "Oh, to make things with," John said. When Toby didn't buy it, John did. On his way out he commented, "You never know when you'll need a knife like this."

CHAPTER FOUR

ON John's ninth birthday an event oc-
curred that would influence his whole life. He was given a copy of
Malory's *Morte d'Arthur*, the first book he ever owned. He reveled in it
and would lie awake at night picturing the gallant knights in armor as
they performed their stirring deeds. Before long, he and Mary were
pretending to be knight and squire and even talked in their own secret
language, using obscure words and terminology from Middle English
times. The Arthurian tales became a passion he never outgrew, sparking
a study of Anglo-Saxon and Middle English and probably affecting his
prose style more than any other book save the King James Version of the
Bible. His life-long absorption in these adventures would lead him to
build one of the most impressive collections of Arthurian books in the
world.

Some day, he decided, he would write his own version of King
Arthur and the knights. Before plunging into that project, however, the
Arthurian influence would become apparent in many of his writings,
notably *Tortilla Flat*. On its very first page he would say: "For Danny's
house was not unlike the Round Table, and Danny's friends were not
unlike the knights in it. . . ." And throughout the delightful tale the
Arthurian tone was maintained.

Two noteworthy events happened in 1912. John made a friend who
would become the Huckleberry Finn of his youth and he received just
about the most wonderful gift imaginable for a boy of ten — a pony. Both
incidents would supply groundwork for fiction.

On an afternoon in early summer he was playing street games with
Mary and several kids when he noticed an unknown boy watching from
the sidelines. The newcomer was deeply suntanned, blond, about his
own age but shorter, his eyes alive with interest. He looked as though he
wanted to play, too, but didn't. Next afternoon the new boy quietly took
up his observation post. At an exciting moment he joined in the fun, but

soon withdrew, feeling, he says now, that he was unwanted. John overcame his own reticence where strangers were concerned and invited him back. No further urging was needed. Almost at once the new boy, Max Wagner, proved himself a hard player, stronger than he looked, with a few tricks of his own, and he implicitly followed all of John's barked commands. Max's parents were American citizens, but he was born and raised in Mexico.

Max and his mother were staying at the home of the boy's grandmother, only a block away. As John pieced together bits of his new friend's life, learning that he had been thrown out of one Mexican school after another for misbehaving, Max took on new importance. He was soon a friend of the entire family — not only of John and Mary, but of John's sister Beth, who would leave later that year for Mills College (where Esther had enrolled two years previously), and of John's parents.

For one reason or another, the Steinbeck reading hours were occasionally skipped during this period, and John, Mary, and Max would sit talking on the front porch steps. Sometimes Mrs. Steinbeck came out with kitchen goodies and casually commented about John's future career. Max gained the impression that she expected her son to enter finance or business. John's father, on the other hand, was never known to hint a preference. John himself was noncommittal.

Whatever it was that started John telling ghost stories is not known, but it might well have been the recent sinking of the *Titanic*, with its "ghost passengers." Or perhaps his tales of spooks, sprites, and other invisible beings stemmed from accounts of leprechauns as told by his Irish kin. Whatever the reason he spun his ghost stories convincingly — and apparently enjoyed them as much as his audience.

"Even as a kid, John was good at this," Max Wagner recalls. "He was always interesting and dramatized everything. Storytelling was natural for him, I guess — not only spooky stuff but other kinds, too. And he made them all up."

Max, in turn, entertained John and Mary on the porch with accounts of Mexico and the boyhood games there. Contrary to John's imaginative turn of mind, Max spoke factually. John asked many questions about the country to the south.

Max's mother, who, like Mrs. Steinbeck, had been a schoolteacher in her younger days, often dropped by to visit John's mother. During one visit, in the presence of John and the others, she turned the conversation to her childhood when her name was Edith Gilfillan. She told of riding the narrow-gauge train from Salinas to Monterey, through fields of fragrant, yellow haystacks, to attend a "free funeral." Wandering away from the funeral rites in the coastal city, she encountered Robert Louis Stevenson. The name of the famous author meant nothing to the little girl at that time. John was fascinated. The tale must have channeled a deep memory groove, for nearly thirty years later he tapped his recollections, changed proper names, and wrote "How Edith McGillcuddy Met R. L. S." (*Harper's Magazine,* 1941). Naturally John sent Max's mother a copy. She answered movingly, but still took him gently to task; his story had pictured her wearing plain black stockings instead of her pretty striped ones!

Some thirty years later, in 1943, John spent several months in the European war zone as a correspondent for the *New York Herald Tribune.* While en route he stopped in London, where he heard a familiar voice on his phone in the Grosvenor House Hotel — it was Max Wagner, private first class, U. S. Air Force Engineers. Stationed in Africa, Max was also briefly staying in London. Within the hour, Max and John were together in the Grosvenor lobby and later in a Fleet Street pub where they reminisced until the closing hour about old times in Salinas.

Pigeons cooed happily at the Treavors place, near John's home. Not only was Mr. Treavors a good provider and nursemaid but a good housekeeper. Noteworthy was the way he kept his backyard cotes free of lice through some unexplained use of tobacco stems, purchased in bulk. The stems were both cheap and powerful — so powerful, Mr. Treavors boasted, they could blast oak stumps right out of California hardpan.

Shortcutting through this neighbor's yard, John mysteriously came into possession of some of the potent tobacco leavings — a whole paper bagful. He couldn't wait to tell Max and Glenn and other friends and invited them to his "opium den," setting the time for later that day. At the appointed hour the youngsters slipped into John's cellar, one by one, rolled their makin's in scraps of newsprint, and lit up, eagerly puffing away. The mass exodus came quickly. Mothers grew alarmed at the sight of their greenish faces, and family doctors had a field day.

Although John eventually resumed smoking, and smoked nearly all of his life, most victims of Steinbeck's *vomitus violentus* avoided tobacco for years. The youngest member of that original band swore he could no longer stand even a pigeon's coo.

By his own admission, John's introduction to sex came about this time — at the age of nine or ten. It happened when his parents, planning to be away for a few days, hired a sitter to look after the children. They underestimated her talents. The girl had only one leg, but she was a good bedroom teacher and John a willing pupil. He said he could never forget how cheerfully she ignored her handicap.

After that, he assertedly prowled the neighborhood for bait — a charge he would later disclaim. Anyway, one Salinas woman reported that whenever he was spotted in the street, the word spread fast and mothers would hustle their daughters indoors for chaste keeping.

Years later in New York Steinbeck indignantly denied such lecherous intents and said that if mothers hid their daughters, it was news to him. "People believe what they want to believe," he said.

John spent much time admiring the horses in the Dashaway Stables, sometimes getting on the backs of the gentler ones. And sometimes he would visit the Sperry Flour Mills on Castroville Street, a half-mile from home, where his father was in charge. Near the main building was a stable surrounded by a large enclosed area, and it was here that Mr. Steinbeck kept the family horses. Occasionally John would be permitted to ride around the corral, for, like most boys of this farming country, he handled horses well.

On a midsummer morning Mr. Steinbeck announced that he had a surprise for his son. He took the boy to the stable and there in a box stall stood a bay pony. An inkling of John's emotions at this momentous event are perhaps reflected in *The Red Pony:* "A red pony colt was looking at Jody out of the stall. . . . Jody's throat collapsed in on itself and cut his breath short." And, "Jody couldn't bear to look at the pony's eyes any more. He gazed down at his hands for a moment, and he asked very shyly, 'Mine?' " As with Jody, John was told that care of the pony (to be named Jill) would be entirely his responsibility — feeding, currying, brushing, keeping the stall clean.

When John received her, Jill was only partly gentled. With the help of Max Wagner, also accomplished with horses, he finished breaking her at the Sperry Mill enclosure. Before and after each session, as a special treat, John would give her an apple and rub her nose, talking to her much as Jody did with Gabilan.

John took eagerly to his new responsibilities, and, unlike his newspaper route, never forgot any of them. Cleaning the stall became a daily ritual. Naturally, throughout his neighborhood, he took on greater stature than ever. Kids in his block begged for rides, but John was selective, basing his decisions largely on principles of barter. He let Glenn ride because he liked Glenn especially well — and Glenn lent him a saddle. He also let Max ride for the sake of friendship — and a pair of chaps. Another boy offered spurs but John was incensed. "No spurs!" he decreed. And no ride either! Sometimes he drove Jill hitched to a two-wheeled wicker cart.

For once the arrival of heavy rains was unwelcome, since they made it necessary for his pony to remain stabled much of the time. But already John was fiddling with an idea for next year. Maybe he would ride Jill in the 1913 rodeo parade, which daily preceded the Wild West show itself — a parade of horsemen from all over the county, their mounts wearing fine hand-tooled saddles and sparkling bridles.

Near the Steinbeck home at Central Avenue and Stone Street, a meandering slough widened into a miniature lake, and upon this inviting body of water John launched a raft he had made from discarded planks and boxes. When the weather was right, he, Max, and Mary would weigh anchor. Sometimes John permitted his two deckhands to do the poling while he stood up front and pretended to be Columbus.

Plop! Smack in the eye! A ball of mud, catapulted from a lath, squarely found its mark and ran streaking down John's face. John wiped at it with his sleeve and swore undying vengeance on the DelConte troops. Lester DelConte and his followers, living three blocks away, were the mortal enemies of the Steinbeck Warriors, and now the two sides were battling across a slimy canal. The mud flew in gobs and chunks and by the shovelful. Some of it was propelled by arm muscle alone and some on the lath catapults, a device introduced by John and quickly adopted by opposing forces. The tides of battle kept turning. Throughout it all, of course, John led what jousting there was, boldly waving a broom handle as a sword during charges and wearing his father's vest as armor. Even some out-of-neighborhood boys joined John's forces, including Skunkfoot Hill, Pickles Moffat, and one or two others. But when the enemy, in turn, drew on reinforcements, John called it unfair. Mary was no sighing Guinevere that day but one of the most ferocious fighters of all, her dress a nightmare of stains.

The battle went down as a high point in the annals of the Steinbeck neighborhood. Just what happened when the combatants reached home was never revealed. But neither side dared forget the foe. Thereafter, when John and Max walked down Central, they would keep a sharp lookout for the enemy, while the smaller Glenn Graves, following, watched for an attack from the rear.

Finally, an unexpected break. John and Max spotted Lester Del-Conte *alone*. Hiding behind some bushes, they sprang out at the right moment, John hissing that Lester was their prisoner of war. The prisoner was hauled into the Steinbecks' cellar, where John trussed him up with rope and tied him to a stanchion. Mary happened in but was told to leave. John warned the captive to remain silent until after the trial, when, depending on the verdict, he would be freed or shot.

The seriousness of the case was discussed in the attic room by John and Max, but the conversation soon drifted from Lester's crimes to sunken treasure ships. This led John to comment on his coin collection. Drawing the blinds and lighting a candle atop a human skull, which he kept conveniently at hand, he produced a cigar box of coins, unmatched poker chips, cigar bands from his uncle, and horseshoe nails, all of which he generously gave to his friend.

From the attic, the two friends descended to the street to join in a baseball game. As evening approached, Max departed and John went home for dinner. During a lull in the table conversation, faint moans were heard coming from under the floor, followed by muffled sounds that resembled crying. Until that moment John had forgotten all about his prisoner of war. Offhandedly he suggested that perhaps their darned cat was trapped in the cellar, but his mother wasn't fooled. Mary held her tongue. Bit by bit, Mrs. Steinbeck dragged out the truth and indignantly ordered the immediate release of that "poor lamb" down there in the dark and cold and missing his dinner.

CHAPTER FIVE

IN her determined efforts to propel John toward a respectable career, his mother applied numerous coats of polish to "civilize" her young son. She wanted him to have not only a knowledge of trade and barter, and appreciation of a dollar, but also an appreciation of culture befitting a man "in finance." ("She wanted me desperately to be something decent like a banker. She would have liked me to be a successful writer like Tarkington but this she didn't believe I could do." — *Journal of a Novel.*)

Her enrichment campaign included periodic trips to The City, as everyone in town called San Francisco. They would board the Southern Pacific train and travel northward in coach seats, finally pulling into The City, a hundred miles from their starting point. To John, the lights, sounds, and crowds of San Francisco were pure magic. Some day, he vowed to himself, he would live in just such a place. Among the concert artists his mother took him to see and hear when he was a "medium-sized kid" — his own description — were Melba, Tetrazzini, Scotti, "and the rest of that fantastic band of archangels." It was a pretty stiff jolt of culture for a boy from a cow town whose live musical diet until then had mostly been Joe Conners singing "When Irish Eyes Are Smiling" and a lady violinist grimly sawing on her fiddle without ever getting it cut in half. The enthralled visitor even got to "see, hear, and touch" Eleonora Duse, and ". . . even though she played Ghosts in Italian, it didn't matter. Even at that age it seemed to me that she brought something to the theater that was lacking in our seasonal Chatauqua or the Salinas High School's version of Mrs. Bumpstead-Leigh." — *San Francisco Examiner.*

Almost as exhilarating as the City by the Golden Gate, but in a vastly different key, were summer vacations and occasional spring weekends spent on the Monterey Peninsula. John would travel there on ponyback in company with his sister Beth or others, while his parents and Mary traveled the twenty miles of roadway by surrey. On the way, the riders would cross the Salinas River bridge, jog between the rolling hills that were so much a part of John's stories, and sometimes stop to picnic on the ranch owned by Aunt Molly Martin in the Corral de Tierra (a valley that became *The Pastures of Heaven*). With their mounts tethered nearby, they would eat on the banks of a lovely stream, watch the quail, perhaps catch the sight of a bounding rabbit, and often gaze upon the sandstone castles caused by erosion in the rock formations some distance away. To John, these towers, turrets, and drawbridges were not make-believe at all but part of his beloved Camelot.

"Sure look real, don't they?" Mary said, also fascinated by the castles.

"Why, they *are* real!" John protested. "See the crowds — see there — the knights and the ladies!"

Mary squinted some more and soon agreed with her imaginative brother.

Reaching the Peninsula, the travelers would ride to a tiny, vine-covered house at 147 Eleventh Street in Pacific Grove, a cottage built by the senior Steinbeck in 1903. The family would swim, fish, hike, and gather ferns and wildflowers.

There is no record of when Jill had a colt, but John described the day as one of the most important in his life. Some hint of the depths to which he was stirred is revealed in *The Red Pony*. Also, there is no record of the day John ultimately parted with Jill or under what circumstances. Just the same, he never forgot this boyhood gift.

As high school enrollment drew near, John spent more and more time alone in his room, adventuring in books. His sister Beth says no restrictions were placed upon his reading, a freedom that led him to a surprising number of classics. Among them were *Crime and Punishment, Madame Bovary*, parts of *Paradise Lost*, some of George Eliot, and *The Return of the Native*. But his tastes were catholic. One volume he treasured was *A Tramp's Life*, stolen from a bookstore. He apparently never did repent, however, the book remaining in his possession to his dying day. The boy Steinbeck was a familiar figure to Mrs. Carrie Streining, the city librarian.

During his pre-adolescent years, John began to show an increasing interest in nature. He often visited the home of his friend Ed Silliman at Alisal and Riker streets, just four blocks from his own house. Ed's father, O. P. Silliman, was a recognized authority on birds. In back of the house was a study and storeroom containing thousands of bird skins and eggs, all neatly filed and catalogued, together with a vast library. John spent many hours with Ed poring over the specimens and books.

In August 1915, when John was thirteen and a half, he entered Salinas High School, a two-story red brick building irreverently called "the brick pile." His class of twenty-seven members swelled the school's total enrollment to about 200.

Throughout his high school career John made slightly better than average grades, a "B" or "B+" in nearly all subjects — English composition and literature, Latin, algebra, plane geometry, chemistry, physics, ancient history, typewriting, U.S. history, Spanish, and government-economics.

His general school deportment was usually rated by his teachers as good." Away from school, however, his behavior was sometimes questioned — by everyone but his mother. Usually she'd close her eyes to his faults, often refusing to admit them even to herself. One such occasion was the night fifteen-year-old John and his friends went on a wine binge. Since the cheap and powerful grappa had a distinct kerosene taste, they decided to play it safe and adopted a rule not to strike a match within three minutes after taking a drink. But that didn't discourage John. He swilled the stuff and, in the process, lost his tie, half his shirt, and all of his dinner. Finally, the world spinning, he reeled homeward, staggered up to ring the doorbell, and collapsed on the porch. His mother, who had been waiting up for him, looked down at her son in dismay.

"Mother," he mumbled, blearily looking up, "I'm drunk."

"No, John," she said firmly, "you're sick!" Even though she knew that he was horribly right, the proprieties wouldn't let her acknowledge it.

"I'm drunk," he repeated.

"No, no, you're sick," she insisted. "Not drunk, *sick!*"

After more words to this effect, neither giving ground, she helped him indoors, quietly cleaned him up as best she could, and put him to bed, careful to avoid any mention of his true condition. John didn't booze it up again for a full two weeks.

Two teachers in high school who fired him with a hunger for knowledge were Ora M. Cupp, who taught English composition and literature, and Emma F. Hawkins, teacher of mathematics and, periodically, chemistry and biology. Miss Hawkins so inspired John that she became the only teacher he ever mentioned in a published work — *The California Teachers Association Journal*, November 1955.

In a letter from San Diego on November 8, 1940, Miss Cupp remembered at length her star pupil:

". . . My guess is that John Steinbeck rated about 120 [estimated I. Q.] (*maybe* more), which is good run of the mill college material — for a good college. . . . In other words, John could have made good in any college, comfortably. That he didn't is due to character traits; not lack of brain power. I say this regardless of any failures or successes, in his later life. I am not able to pass judgment on his adaptability.

"In English John was college material and could do good work when he felt inclined. Note that his grade was cut because he didn't hand in required work. No argument in the world would have made John hand in that work if he decided not to. I sometimes thought John would have been glad to have someone help him unmake-up his mind, but of course no one could. I am not sure John could himself, even then. It might have been my fault about the missing papers; it might have been John's mood.

"John was violent where a 'stuffed shirt' was concerned, and he didn't mind being loud or rude while he 'told the world.' I think one could feel his power to hate even while he was still in short pants, and in the "grubby state" of boyhood.

"He hadn't much opportunity to show the following trait in the classroom, but I was conscious then of its potentiality. He was likely to side with anyone that he thought was not getting a square deal, and to be noisy in delivering his views. Even so, I felt I sometimes caught him with his tongue in his cheek, and he knew I'd caught him though neither one of us said a word.

"May I digress here a moment? I've wondered often whether his tongue was in his cheek as he wrote some of his books. These people were 'good copy'; let the reader cry over them if he or she liked. Of course Life had done a good many things to him by that time, or he thought it had, and what was only a tendency in the boy *may* have become set, like plaster of Paris, in the man. Even though the tendency had become set in his adult-hood, I'm willing to wager there were times when he stood off and grinned at his own indignation. He always dropped his eyes and grinned when he was caught at this — in his kid-hood.

"I am told that John grew very bitter toward society between his college days and the time of his final recognition by editors and reading public. Query: was that bitterness so deep seated that it became permanent, or will money and recognition affect his viewpoint? If so, what may we expect from his pen in the future? If he writes in the same vein, here's one person who'll wager a doughnut that his tongue will be in his cheek all the time when he isn't completely lost in the composition of his story. And I believe he'd still drop his eyes and grin at being caught.

"There were symptoms of the introvert in John in his high school days. That's often true of adolescents, but is generally a passing phase. I've wondered if a certain bashfulness, concealed by swagger, might have been at the bottom of it. For there was something in John that was highly sensitive, and I don't think it was pride, then. Something happened to him; else the Stanford history would have been different.

"It has been said that the death of Mrs. Martin, his aunt, may have had a profound influence on John's career. . . . She was childless, and devoted to Mrs. Steinbeck's children. Mr. Steinbeck kept his children — his family — nicely, but probably had little left over for college expenses. When Mrs. Martin died, naturally Mr. Martin hadn't the same interest in the Steinbecks; he remarried, became the father of a child, and died, leaving nothing to his wife's family — his first wife's family. John had been promised much by his aunt. He got nothing. . . . John may have felt that his college fees were a drain on the family. After all, a blow to an adolescent boy is often very serious in its consequences. What *did* cause him to leave Stanford? A Stanford student told me that John seemed not to fit in, retired into himself more and more, and left. Things had to change greatly for the boy of 1915-16-17, else the Stanford history would have been impossible.

"You asked about pranks. I think John played plenty of tricks in his school days, but he was in a crowded class with many bright and able youngsters, all of them full of the ginger and general 'cussedness' of youth, which all teachers expect, and really enjoy behind the necessary school teachery frown. None of these children was (or were) bad; so I don't remember any particular escapade. I rarely remembered the antics of even the *very* bad child, and I had a few of those in Salinas. John was never bad in the sense of being mean or hard to control. No doubt I scolded him, probably 'bawled him out,' maybe cut his deportment record, etc., but I am glad I never had a class of perfect children to teach. It would have been deadly dull if I hadn't had to be on the alert all the time. I can understand the comment of one of pupils here in San Diego about *Paradise Lost.* 'Gee, it must be dull in Heaven if the angels are all perfect since Lucifer got kicked out! . . .' "

During high school John lost some of his boyhood reticence and got along fairly well with most of his classmates. He showed an interest in student government, participated in sports, and was right guide in a student cadet company. (Max Wagner was a top sergeant.) He had little use for pretentiousness, however, whether in his peers or in the faculty. He could listen to heated arguments for only a limited time before he joined in, usually on the weaker side.

One of his classmates was Ignatius Cooper, the school's only black student, whose father ran a small trucking business, and his mother " . . . was a warm and friendly woman who was good for a piece of gingerbread any time we wanted to put the hustle on her. . . . If there was any color prejudice in Salinas I never heard of it." Still further, ". . . . Ignatius, my classmate, was not my favorite. I discover now, because he was far and away the best student. In arithmetic and later in mathematics he topped our grades, and in Latin he not only was a better student, but he didn't cheat. And who can like a classmate like that?" — *Journal of a Novel.*

For his part, Ignatius remembers John as "the type that meant what he said — he was that way all his life. If he didn't like you, he would tell you so." He describes John in high school as being of medium size and a good student, but not much of an athlete, and concludes, "As far as I know, he didn't do much writing."

On the last score Ignatius Cooper was mistaken. He didn't know about the writing simply because John never discussed it. Sometime during his high school career he had begun penning compositions at home, not only for school but for his own satisfaction. An item he wrote for the school yearbook, as undistinguished as it may be, reveals his tongue-in-cheek attitude:

"When the Student Body of a school runs smoothly, it is a good sign that the school is in good order. The Student Body is really the center of school life. All amusements and all obligations swing upon it, and our Student Body *is* running smoothly. This does not mean with a lack of interest for there is always interest. In fact, the interest ran so high just before the Salinas-Santa Cruz basket ball game that Main Street had to be cleared to keep things from being broken. Truly, ours is a Student Body to be proud of because it does things. At every contest this year, the Student Body has been almost unanimously represented. Pep and cooperation have been our motto and we have lived up to it. The pep rose to such an extent that a mallet had to be made to call the assembly to order. — J.S., '19."

Without a word to anyone, save possibly Mary, young Steinbeck often worked far into the night in his slant-ceilinged attic room. Mrs. Graves across the street, on occasions when she was awake at one or two in the morning, said she always saw a rectangular glow of light in an upstairs Steinbeck window.

Years later, in a letter to Dorothy Vera, John wrote: ". . . your speaking of the old house on Central Avenue reminded me. . . . I used to sit in that little room upstairs . . . and write little stories and little pieces and send them out to magazines under a false name and I never put a return address on them. . . . I wonder what I was thinking of? I was scared to death to get a rejection slip, but more, to get an acceptance."

In *Journal of a Novel*, possibly in reference to a morning after a late night session, he said, "This is a grey day but the kind I like. Reminds me of mornings in Salinas when I hated to get up and go to school."

In an unguarded moment, right out of the azure, he said to his classmate, John Murphy, "You know, I write the purest English of anybody in the world." When he apparently realized how his comment must have sounded, he flushed and quickly changed the subject. Murphy commented long afterward that John must have been writing then and, further, he must have sensed he wasn't doing badly. To him, the story line, the sound and meaning of words, originality, a tale's "texture" and rhythm were all-important.

On a stairwell in high school hung a large framed sepia print of a knight in armor, visor closed, the gift to the school of some graduating class. Murphy occasionally came upon John standing on the stairs gazing at the picture, almost in a trance. Sometimes Murphy brushed past his friend without ever being noticed.

In the spring of 1918 John suffered his first serious illness. Coming home from school one day, he complained of feeling poorly and was put to bed. The thermometer was alarming, and Dr. Murphy was called.

His illness, pleural pneumonia, grew worse in a savage hurry. Soon burning with fever, irrational, and in need of constant attention, he sank to such dangerous lows that his mother and nurses were kept on constant duty. John's father frequently sat up with his son throughout the night, even though he had put in a full day's work. John's older sisters were away — Beth living in New York, Esther teaching in Watsonville — so that thirteen-year-old Mary, badly frightened, did much of the housework.

Concerned neighbors, friends, and relatives offered help, and the family's Episcopal minister prayed for the stricken youth, as did the nuns of a nearby convent. "I went down and down," said Steinbeck in *East of Eden*, "until the wing tips of the angels brushed my eyes." Dr. Murphy was obviously worried. Sixteen years before he had ushered in this life; he swore now by all the saints and Hippocrates himself that he wouldn't usher it out. He called in a consultant, and drastic steps were undertaken. They removed a rib and inserted a drain to take the pus from the pleural cavity, an operation performed at home. Word went out to others of this closely knit clan and they started converging on Salinas.

As the crisis neared, the nurses gently tried to prepare John's father

44

and mother for the worst. But the quiet, self-possessed father was not to be shaken; he had a premonition — he *knew* — that his son would weather the terrible illness. Alone with Esther, he laid his hand upon her arm and said confidently, "John is going to live!" The crucial turning point neared, and John safely passed it. When John was able to return to his familiar quarters upstairs, it was not long until his nighttime attic window glowed regularly again with a yellowish light — a sign to wakeful Mrs. Graves that all was right once more in the Steinbeck world.

John's illness had kept him confined to bed for nine weeks, and when he regained his strength he found that he had three months of school work to make up. During his illness had he ever feared dying? The answer was no. In a conversation with his buddy, Ed Silliman, he matter of factly stated he held little regard for his own life, but would never consider suicide. It was just that he didn't care about "being," a view further borne out in *Journal of a Novel* when he said, "I have no will to die but I can remember no time from earliest childhood when I would not have preferred never to have existed. . . . You see it is no longing for death but a kind of hunger never to have lived."

John took a number of different jobs during his high school years, usually on ranches. For a time he was a rodman with a survey party on the old Monterey Road. Another time he was an oiler on a dredger draining lakes and canals near Castroville, a few miles from Salinas. R. B. Cozzens, superintendent of the Granite Rock Company connected with the project, recalls that John camped beside the road with other workmen, but ate at the little Bennet Hotel in Castroville. Room and board there cost a dollar a day, and single meals went at twenty-five and thirty cents, depending on appetite. John took the deluxe plate. He could afford it. He earned $2.50 a day. A regular customer at the Bennet Hotel was a dim-witted gorilla of a man whose hairy hands swung from powerful arms and nearly reached his knees. Cozzens is convinced that this awesome boarder became John's prototype for the titular role in *Johnny Bear* and for Lenny in *Of Mice and Men*.

At the Spreckels sugar factory, where he worked briefly at a manual job, he got metal filings in his eyes and was taken home with both eyes bandaged. The accident caused no permanent damage. During his brief time off his steady companion was Jiggs, part bulldog, with a comical black-ringed eye. John got off easier that time than he did in June 1963 when, on Long Island, he underwent surgery for a detached retina of the left eye. The operation was successful, but for once he was caught without a dog, his famous Charley having died only the month before.

John's senior year in Salinas held several distinctions. He was elected president of his class and also played a part in the school play, *Mrs. Bumpstead-Leigh*, which was performed in White's Theater on Main Street to accommodate the crowds. He played the minor role of Justin Rawson, and when he went on stage he barely remembered his only line, "Just in time." The editorship of the school yearbook, *El Gabilan*, went to another, but John was appointed an associate editor. Jointly he and Nima Dill were in charge of "Departments and Organizations." His first full-length published writing, "The How, When and Where of the High School," appeared in the 1919 *El Gabilan*, excerpted here:

"The English room, which is just down the hall from the office, is the sanctuary of Shakespeare, the temple of Milton and Byron, and the terror of Freshmen. English is a kind of high brow idea of the American language. A hard job is made of nothing at all and nothing at all is made of a hard job. It is in this room and this room alone, that the English language is spoken. After taking English for four years we wish to advise Freshmen to use nothing but second hand books; they make the course much easier. . . ."

In *El Gabilan's* "Class Prognostications," associate editor Hazel Carpenter looked into her crystal globe and foresaw a preacher's life for John.

> The church of a far-off city
> Came towering into view,
> Where John was preaching in solemn tones
> To many a well-filled pew.

John, however, had no intention of turning to the pulpit. Instead, toying with different plans, he listed on a questionnaire the college of his choice. And spelled it *Standford*.

CHAPTER SIX

O N an unseasonably warm October day in 1919, the husky youngster from Salinas in the new, ill-fitting clothes lightly swung his suitcase and himself from Palo Alto's University Avenue streetcar and onto the Stanford campus. At long last the time had come to see if the academic whetstone could sharpen his writing skill. Sometimes he was buoyed up by the belief that he had considerable talent and frankly, without vanity, said so — and at other times he admitted to an almost unbearable fear that this whole dream was a damned lie. Before long, he'd know, for he had all but decided to make writing his career — writing of almost any sort.

As he walked from the trolley tracks on that registration day, an eagerly awaited scene spread before him — a scatter of yellow sandstone buildings snuggled against low-lying hills, inviting walks and archways, and hurrying knots of arriving students. But there was little time to look around. Two luggage-toting sophomores ahead of him caught his attention. They called to him. He stepped forward. One of them sized up the husky lad from the country and brusquely ordered him to help with their bags. He made no move to comply. The shorter of the pair arrogantly repeated the order, adding the word "rube." At that, Steinbeck brushed past them and strode to Encina Hall, quickly climbed the stone steps of the five-story men's dormitory, and vanished through an arched entrance — unheard-of-treatment of mighty sophomores by a lowly freshman.

Stowing his suitcase in his assigned room on the first floor, No. 111, he headed for the men's outdoor swimming pool. It didn't take long to shuck his clothes in the adjoining gym and jackknife naked into the water. Tanned and solid, appearing a bit older than his seventeen years, the six-footer raced another swimmer and won easily. His competitor turned out to be a freshman his own age, and soon they were seated at the pool's edge, getting acquainted.

His new friend was George L. Mors of Los Gatos, California, who said he would be majoring in mechanical engineering but expressed considerable interest in the military. In answer to a question, John said he was going to be a journalist. Rather than draw an unknown roommate, John suggested they room together. Mors agreed and soon moved into No. 111, a cubicle larger than most, with white-painted walls and a minimum of furniture. Before long John installed a caged canary and a small aquarium of goldfish, each of which was given a name of its own.

As Mors chatted, John haphazardly transferred his belongings from suitcase to bureau. Atop the bureau he placed his shaving gear and a mirror, the glass reflecting a face that by Hollywood standards was anything but handsome — a plain, strong-featured face, ears seeming larger than ever, nose large and broad — "my big blob of a nose," he called it — blue eyes and full lips. His curly dark brown hair, clipped high and close around the temples, emphasized the height of his forehead and breadth of his face at the cheekbones. Although he grinned now and then, and laughed hard when something tickled him, his expression for the most part was serious. Mors, for his part, laid out his possessions with meticulous care, precisely adjusted the angle of his own mirror, shook the wrinkles from his coat before hanging it up, and moved about with army snap.

During the first hectic weeks on campus, in the course of discussions with his instructors, the contradictory aspects of John's nature became apparent. Although he was outwardly timid, rebellion simmered not far below the surface. He pleaded against taking certain required courses. Why, he wanted to know, should he be forced to attend classes that, for him, were only so much excess baggage? Why did the school insist on feeding him subjects for which he had no taste? He was going to be a writer. Let him take classes that might help him, that might advance him in his chosen field. His arguments — even his veiled threats to "walk out" — sounded strikingly like those of students two generations later, but all efforts failed. In the end, and even though the discipline was galling, he did exactly as directed that first year, taking some mandatory courses and some electives. Later on in his college career he would prove to be more successful at getting his own way. His freshman courses were composition, English history, elementary French, mental hygiene, nineteenth century painters, American history, elementary economics, English literature (from Malory to Browning), and two military science courses.

The initial rush at Stanford subsided after a few weeks, and a reasonable routine set in. John explored the campus and liked what he saw. Most academic activity, he found, centered in buildings forming a quadrangle, known as the Quad, the sandstone structures topped with red tile. The walks around both the outer and inner Quad were rimmed by graceful arches, and there were occasional benches where one could sit to think things out or chat with some acquaintance. Most of all, he liked the quiet of the inner Quad, where grass plots and flower beds fronted the famous chapel, with its facade of colorful mosaic. No wonder Stanford was called "The Farm," a name going back to the days when wealthy Senator Leland Stanford raised trotting horses and other blooded stock on his land. The farm-like serenity persisted.

Although funds from home provided necessities, there was little left over. John lived comfortably but frugally. Occasionally, to cut expenses, he and George would walk through the hushed evening campus to Palo Alto for a thirty-five cent dinner at the City Cafe, a Chinese restaurant popular among students. Sometimes on these jaunts they would encounter other students they knew and stop to speak, but by and large John was a loner. His not mixing, or mixing with caution, even in classrooms did not win him many friends. Being a semi-recluse was simply his nature, something he was painfully aware of, but could do little about. One classmate he did get to know slightly that first semester was Carlton (Dook) Sheffield, an English major from Long Beach, California, who years later recalled their meeting:

"Sometime during the fall of 1919, I became aware of a large, quiet classmate who entered the school at the time I did. Together we were enrolled in a class in elementary French, and beyond the fact that his name was Steinbeck and that he seemed unhappy when called upon to recite, I knew nothing about him. But he had one outstanding physical characteristic. When he laughed, one suddenly noticed how blue his eyes were and what an intense sparkle they had — they seemed to dance with delight when something pleased him. Well, we nodded when we met, and once in a while exchanged pungent views on the absurdities of French grammar and punctuation, but that was about the extent of it, though we both lived in Encina Hall."

Striken with influenza during his second quarter at Stanford, John was granted a temporary leave of absence and went home, but was back again for the spring of 1920 and resumed rooming with Mors. Not long after his return, as he walked down a corridor of E-shaped Encina, he passed the short, stocky sophomore of opening day. Neither seemed to notice the other, but as John entered his room he felt Shorty watching.

George Mors was not in. Steinbeck grew vaguely uneasy as he sat down at his desk to study. Would a knock come? It didn't. Instead the door opened and in filed four sophomores, the short one leading the way.

Shorty spoke three words: "Come with us."

John spoke two: "Not today."

He had been expecting something like this and was prepared. From a drawer he pulled a long-barreled .45 Smith & Wesson and shoved it on the desk in front of him. The visitors stopped. After a whispered conference and many sidelong glances, they decided against intruding and retired, muttering threats of retaliation. Although the gun was reported to have lacked a firing pin, it looked vicious enough to blast holes in hordes. The incident did nothing to increase John's popularity.

Just the same, he must have wondered if he would encounter Shorty in the Tie-Up, a traditional interclass battle. In the Tie-Up the freshmen and sophomores faced each other on the football field, each man armed with short lengths of rope. At a signal the gladiators tried to hog-tie opponents. The side taking the most captives won. For military-minded George, this must have been a rare fun sport, with its charges, feints, deployments, and final siege. There is no record of John and Shorty having tangled, but, if they did, John apparently escaped unscathed, for he and George looked forward to next year's melee. At least a 1920 photograph of the sophomore class of that year, taken just before the Tie-Up, shows John and George Mors with rope dangling from their belts and their elbows locked, both grinning in anticipation. The photo also provides a tip-off to the independence and inventiveness that were to become so strikingly pronounced in the mature Steinbeck. Though the 200 youths behind them in the picture are fully, though disreputably, dressed, young Steinbeck and Mors are naked from the waist up, a gross immodesty in that generation. Both are, moreover, thoroughly greased to make their capture more difficult. Every surrounding face is turned toward the two innovators with laughing astonishment, admiration, or amused disapproval. (Stripping for action was one thing, but being *photographed* that way was almost going too far.) Even so, their adaptation of a carnival's greased-pig ploy set a popular precedent.

During that first year John ached to get into sports. He tried out for the freshman football team, but didn't make it. In R.O.T.C. polo he cracked a kneecap, an injury which was to give him lifelong trouble. Years later in New York he seriously redamaged this knee when an outside balcony railing gave way and he crashed to the sidewalk below.

Needing some extra money about this time, John hunted part-time work and found a night job as waiter in Palo Alto's City Cafe. The number of dishes he broke brought only mild protests, but gradually misunderstandings developed with one of the temperamental Chinese cooks. Finally one evening the disagreements flared into an open feud, and, screaming insults, the cook grabbed up a cleaver. Apron billowing, John flew toward the door leading into the restaurant proper, and so did the murderous weapon. In his own version, he and the cleaver reached there simultaneously, the blade sticking in the doorjam. While the startled diners looked on, John continued into the street, tearing off his apron en route and flinging it into the entryway. He never went back.

When returning on foot to Encina Hall from dinner in Palo Alto or a night movie there, most students usually stopped beside a certain towering and friendly eucalyptus tree for bladder relief. Always the same ritual, always the same tree. The patient old tree had performed its service through the years and was affectionately referred to by initials only, T.L.S.J.U.O.P.T. — "The Leland Stanford Junior University Official Pissing Tree."

One moonlit night as John and others ringed its trunk, they heard a woman's footsteps approaching. It was Margery Bailey, an English instructor. They could see her clearly. The walk to her campus home from Palo Alto would bring her within a few yards of them, but the embarrassed boys kept right on obeying nature's call. Nearer and nearer she came. She drew abreast, pretending not to notice, but when some distance beyond, she slowed down a little and called back: "For once I wish I were a man."

By the spring of 1920, the friendship of John and Dook Sheffield extended beyond the French class, and occasionally Dook went to John's room for a few rounds of boxing practice. They would move back the table and chairs, don gloves and start trading punches, with George Mors refereeing. Dook invariably got the worst of it, for John had greater height, reach, weight, and skill, together with cat-like movements which made most of his blows totally unexpected. On the other hand, Dook adds, his opponent fought considerately, always trying to keep his punches from being too punishing and never taking unfair advantage.

An attack of acute appendicitis early in May put John in the hospital for surgery and out of commission for the remainder of the spring term. Recuperating in Salinas, he soon regained his strength and began looking for summer work. With the help of his father, both he and George Mors were promised jobs as rodmen with a location-survey camp in the Big Sur district of Monterey County, near the coast where scenic Highway 1 would eventually run. The work of a rodman was a "cinch," John explained to Mors — rodmen simply held up poles for the surveyor. The region was remote, wild, and rugged, but John's mother, many years before his birth, had taught in a tiny schoolhouse there.

While waiting for Mors to join him in Salinas (Mors was busy finding caretakers for the canary and goldfish), John had a chance to review his school record. What a rotten start! The spring semester was a gaping hole. Too much illness. From October 1, 1919, until about May 20, 1920, he had satisfactorily completed only three courses for ten units, getting a C in composition, a C- in a second composition course, and a B in English history. All other grades were inconclusive, such as "Incomplete," "Withdrew," or "Conditional."

The first day on the job at the survey camp the new rodmen found their jobs not quite the cinch predicted. Besides lugging the surveying rods, they dragged chains and hacked away brush — chaparral and thornbush as unyielding as barbed wire. Thorns tore at their flesh, axe handles raised blisters, poison oak added to the misery. Things went from bad to worse when it was chow time, but at least meals were consistent — always terrible. The lunches, packed in old Union Leader tobacco boxes, invariably consisted of a wormy apple, two slices of bread, a can of salmon, and a stale piece of cake. Both boys came to dread noontime and coveted the lavish lunches prepared exclusively for the boss, whose wife was camp cook.

"What damn lousy jobs we got!" said John. "Every day gets worse."

"Yeah," George agreed, "and it was your idea. 'Easy work,' you called it."

John ignored the sarcasm. "What gets me," he said bitterly, "are the camp suppers. I never ate worse."

"You like the lunches better?" George chided.

When John's father sent word that his son could work at Spreckels near Salinas if he preferred, John accepted at once and managed to line up another job there for George. For the rest of the summer, Mors lived in the Steinbeck home and worked with John at the Spreckels sugar factory, which they would reach after a twenty-minute ride on the narrow-gauge railroad. The beet sugar factory, largest in the world, consisted of several cavernous, red-brick buildings clustered in the company town of Spreckels. John used hammer and saw while George carried hod, though both were listed as "carpenter's helpers." Compared with the survey camp, it was paradise. They worked nine hours a day, six days a week, and earned $100 a month.

John's father, soon to become county treasurer, also worked in the sugar mill, something he'd done since leaving the flour mill and after selling his feed store. Seated at a desk in the main building, Mr. Steinbeck made card entries of storeroom supplies, his shoulders hunched over his work, blue eyes squinting. He looked somewhat like his son, but there the similarity ended; unlike maverick John, he was not one to stir up resentments. At noontime, following lunch at his desk, the father was privileged to wander outside and putter among the flowers in his personal garden beside the experimental station, a plot authorized by his lifelong friend, the resident manager. At day's end, and regardless of a yardful of flowers at home, Mr. Steinbeck would often take home a bouquet for his wife, invariably presenting it with a courtly bow.

After dinner one evening, when Mrs. Steinbeck had left for a meeting of the Wanderers' Club, the elder Steinbeck, his son, fifteen-year-old daughter Mary, and George gathered in the high-ceilinged, book-lined sitting room. For awhile, John played both classical and popular tunes on the massive Edison phonograph, including "After You've Gone," "Dardanella" and some Caruso records. The four discussed the scandalous heights to which skirts had climbed, six inches above the ground! Then Mr. Steinbeck made an important announcement. As Worshipful Master of Masons and an active parent in school affairs, he had been appointed to assist in the laying of a cornerstone at the new high school. Soon he would want a collection of local products in token amounts to place within it — "so that people a hundred years from now will know how we lived." Would the boys lend him a hand? They would.

On their next day off, the two youths went to work assembling the native commodities, John going about it carelessly, George methodically. Their collection included a handful of dried beans, a few shriveled kernels of corn, a pillbox of sugar, and a gallon of red wine. Alone in John's room, they laid out their wares. John thoughtfully eyed the jug of fermented juice. Since a full gallon plainly exceeded requirements, he went into whispered conference with George and soon dribbled an ounce or two of it into a small medicine bottle for the cornerstone, the jug itself vanishing into a closet.

Mr. Steinbeck, beaming as he entered the room, expressed pleasure at the lineup of items. But he balked at the intoxicant, mildly protesting that wine seemed hardly appropriate for a school cornerstone, especially during prohibition times. John argued to the contrary. If ever there was a *local* product, the son maintained, this was it. And in that, he was right, for Salinas was notoriously a wide-open town where anything went, a point robustly emphasized more than thirty years later in *East of Eden*. His arguments must have been convincing. Mr. Steinbeck began to waver and at last reluctantly agreed to include the sample of wine. In private, the youths hauled out the jug for an advance ceremony of their own. During the schoolyard ritual Mr. Steinbeck managed to maneuver the vial of dago red — stoppered airtight — into the sacred depository. And there it probably is to this day, pleasantly mellowing in the cozy darkness as it awaits the archaeologist's pick.

Mors remembers how John worshiped his sister Mary, looking after her with great concern. She was also a delight to Mors — "a truly bright light in that house." Excitedly she spoke about her own forthcoming enrollment at Stanford. It was a frightening day when Mary fell ill and was confined to her room. The doctor came daily. John refused to leave the house while she was sick. Then, as swiftly as the malady had struck, it left.

"I never learned the diagnosis," Mors says, "but it afforded a good opportunity to see how much John thought of her. He behaved like a faithful dog whose master is hurt."

Believing that an outing might benefit Mary, the family and George prepared for a Sunday visit to the Monterey Peninsula. Before leaving Salinas, young Steinbeck insisted on taking along a gunnysack. He wouldn't explain why. On reaching the peninsula, he told George they would each also need a long stick. Again he acted mysteriously.

While the others were busy elsewhere, the two companions found a pine-studded tract surrounded by old homes, a piney stretch, George says, similar to forest scenes destined for *Tortilla Flat*, particularly the one involving Danny's friends and Pilon on St. Andrew's Eve. Making sure he was within sight of the bordering homes, John dropped to his hands and knees and crawled forward, stick in hand, directing his friend to do likewise. Whenever he came upon a pine cone, John whacked it violently with his stick, hurled it into the sack, twisted the sack closed, and looked for another. To George this smacked of sheer idiocy, but, at John's whispered urgings, he shed his dignity and imitated the silly maneuver. He could see householders peering from behind their curtains. The youths would find more pine cones; then, *whap, whap, whap,* and into the sack! This went on and on. Sweat poured from their faces. George wanted to quit, but John wouldn't. Finally, with fully a dozen pine cones bagged, they carried the sack alongside a house and peeked around the corner. John motioned for silence.

Presently a householder emerged and walked among the trees, apparently trying to find out what the youths had been doing. Frustrated, he returned indoors, only to be imitated by others down the block. Some of them argued among themselves.

Meanwhile, John was enjoying the scene. Mors recalls John's comment: "When a young person does something a little different, older folks always come farting around trying to figure out what he's up to — and when they can't find out, they get mad. Pine cones sure gave us swell bait."

CHAPTER SEVEN

WHEN John returned to school in the autumn of 1920, he and Mors again roomed together, chaperoned by the retrieved goldfish (a turtle had been added), the canary, and a recently purchased chipmunk. From the beginning, young Steinbeck seemed uneasy. Obviously something was worrying him. He signed up for only English classics, elementary French, and military training, or twelve units.

Even so, he still wanted more time for reading. He haunted the Timothy Hopkins Room at the library, neglecting classes, his "big blob of a nose" forever in a book. He read so widely and so much on his own that later he was never able to tell with certainty when he had encountered a particular author, whether before, during, or after the Stanford period. Always he showed eager interest in contemporary writers, including Dreiser, Sherwood Anderson, Norman Douglas, Donn Byrne, Sinclair Lewis, and especially James Branch Cabell. Other writers he enjoyed were Browning, Milton, George Eliot, Thackeray, Jeffers, D.H. Lawrence, Stevenson, O. Henry, Lewis Carroll, Hardy, Dostoyevsky, and Flaubert. Katherine Mansfield and Chekhov were high among his preferences. Greek and Roman mythology intrigued him, and of course his interest in the Arthurian legends never wavered.

Sometimes he pored over the Bible, whose poetic beauty and style he thought magnificent. To him, the Parables were penned in the simplest and purest English on record, and the Book of Job was masterful; its rich and rhythmic style moved him profoundly. He studied Scripture as literature rather than for its religious significance. Indeed, despite his Episcopalian Sunday school upbringing, his religious leanings, if any, remain in doubt. While at Stanford he was never known to attend church or chapel. At one point he was overheard arguing with a purveyor of religious tracts against the existence of a Supreme Being, which actually proved nothing since he liked to argue for the sake of argument. At another point he was talked into going to church by a friend's mother and became so vocally contradictory to the pastor during the sermon that he was all but invited to leave, an event at considerable variance with his enjoyment of hell-and-brimstone services during *Travels With Charley*. One stand he consistently took was to deride virgin births; he branded each of them, whatever the faith, a convenient hoax. And he delighted in the title of a senior student's thesis at Stanford on this very subject — *Phallus in Wonderland*. Despite the conflicting evidence on Steinbeck's innermost beliefs, however, there is no denying that he was well prepared to make telling use of biblical themes, their language and symbolism.

Never one to turn down a glass, Steinbeck showed a good deal of initiative when supplies ran low. One day he entered the room swinging a gallon jug of amber liquid.

"It's sweet cider," John explained to Mors. "We'll age it — and have ourselves some applejack — good ol' hard stuff with a wallop. You'll see."

He disappeared from the room, but was back in a few minutes with a galvanized pail he had filched from a closet in the hall. He gave the bucket to Mors to clean while he made other less strenuous preparations. Carefully he poured the cider into the bucket, setting it on top of the radiator to hasten fermentation.

Thereafter, day after day, the first thing he did on entering the room was to glance into the pail.

"It's coming along great," he'd crow. "Ripening fast. I can hardly wait."

Later on, as the liquid began changing color, he would say, "It's mellowing."

Before long, however, Mors noticed that something appeared to be not quite right. Something seemed to be stirring in the depths of the now murky liquid. Bubbles were arising. Strong odors filled the room. At last came tasting day. John poked a finger into the bucket and touched his lips. He nearly vomited.

"Wonder what's gone wrong," he gasped.

What went wrong, they found out later, was strictly due to a chemical reaction. The galvanized bucket had laced the cider with soluble zinc salts, a dangerous brew. Had they drunk it, they would have become frightfully sick — or died.

Sadly they dumped the whole mess into the toilet, their noble experiment ended. They were surprised it didn't eat away the bowl's enamel.

Classwork took up little of Steinbeck's time that semester, and he was frequently to be found prowling Palo Alto or hiking in the countryside. Classrooms took little of his time. Once, unseen, Dook Sheffield unexpectedly came upon him lying flat on his back near summer-dry Lake Lagunita. Arms folded behind his head, an open book beside him, John was apparently daydreaming as he watched some wisps of clouds. The scene fastened onto Dook's memory — the lake basin, a nearby spring-fed pool, and, closer still, a fine old oak with an oddly twisted lower limb. John appeared oblivious to everything but the sky. ("High in a pale blue sky, a cloud feather or two floated, and on top of the mountain there were several playing about slowly." — "Fingers of Cloud," *The Stanford Spectator*). Dook silently withdrew.

Fellow students pointed out the dire consequences of his lack of interest in his studies, but John would irritably brush them off — and likely as not go striding off somewhere. Those walks, a lifelong habit, came to indicate he faced some problem, either personal or literary. And walks in that semester became more and more frequent.

One Sunday morning, George Mors, a sound sleeper, woke up late to find a note on the stand beside the bed. He was sitting on the edge of his cot, staring at the message uncomprehendingly, when Dook Sheffield came in with a set of boxing gloves, explaining that he and John had a date for a few rounds of sparring, Mors held out the note, saying he had just awakened. Dook took it and read it aloud:

"Gone to China — see you again sometime. Please free the chipmunk."

Most of John's belongings had vanished — clothes, typewriter, luggage, blankets, some of his books and miscellany. The bird cage was open, but the chipmunk, Chipper, revolved in his cage and the fish and turtle lazily moved in the small aquarium on the window ledge. John had evidently come home when George was sound asleep, packed in utmost silence, freed the bird, written the note, and tiptoed out.

George could only guess the reason for leaving. He recalled his roommate's recent restlessness. But why had John left? Mors felt that John simply wanted to get away before he flunked out, not that he would have minded for himself but his love of family was such that he couldn't bear hurting them — as if jumping school were an answer! But Mors' theory was right.

Sometime during late autumn John had been advised by the dean that his academic record was in jeopardy. John had simply been too neglectful of classwork. What effect the dean's edict had upon the supersensitive youth can only be imagined.

"I don't think I ever told you this," John says in *Journal of a Novel,* "but once in college I went flibberty geblut and got to going to the library and reading what I wanted instead of what was required. I got behind and then I got so far behind that I could not possibly catch up. And I still have bad dreams about that. It must have cut a very deep channel."

On December 31, 1920, after John had already left school, he was officially "requested to withdraw from the university". This belated notification went to his high school principal as well as his parents, something that must have caused further pangs when young Steinbeck eventually learned of it.

On the morning of John's disappearance, the aquarium was given to a student who wanted it. That afternoon Dook went to room 424. George Mors was away. Finding the door unlocked, Dook went in and looked around. As usual Chipper was operating his Ferris wheel. The visitor knew precisely what he would do. He carried the cage containing Chipper to Lake Lagunita, skirted it, and approached the old oak tree with the strangely twisted lower limb. Setting the cage on the ground, he opened its door and stepped back. At first the chipmunk, spread-eagled against the bars, remained frozen in fear, but presently sensed freedom and darted out. Once in the field, the small animal became a blurred streak that wavered once, then tore for the oak. Dook saw him climb, but the next instant the image was gone. Well, at least Chipper could dine on acorns that night.

Torn between misgivings and duty fulfilled, Dook made his way back to Encina, idly swinging the empty cage as he went and wondering where Steinbeck was at that moment.

They wouldn't see one another for two years.

Reaching San Francisco, Steinbeck tried to find a ship, but inexperienced seamen were simply not being signed on, even as cabin boys. For weeks he tramped the waterfront without luck. Money ran low. If he communicated with his parents or sisters — a debatable point — he evidently didn't give his address.

During the Christmas shopping rush he clerked at Capwell's department store in Oakland and later worked in a haberdashery. Moving southward, he stopped briefly in Los Gatos, George Mors's hometown. In a letter to Mors long afterward he said, "I was remembering how I jumped school and hid out in your mother's grocery. She must have hated it. And I remember all the foolish lies I told."

Resuming his southward trek, he passed through several drab little towns, working as a laborer and ranch hand as he went. Once in the Salinas area he skirted his hometown and eventually found a job on what is believed to be the Willoughby Ranch, Spreckels Ranch No. 10 — a job that was to become extremely important to his literary career. The big ranch was between Spence and Chualar, its western section devoted to beet fields, while barley grew on the sloping higher ground to the east. Here, bucking bags of grain, living in the bunkhouse with the men, he worked hard and soon rose to straw boss. Among the hired hands was an ancient, one-armed stable roustabout and squirrel poisoner whom Steinbeck fans would get to know as "the old swamper."

On the big ranch he tried his hand at several pieces of fiction. It is likely that he mulled over a hundred stories, though he was to tell Dook that he "didn't think at all." If not thinking through plots he most certainly was absorbing more color and feel for this part of the already familiar Salinas Valley — the sunny and friendly Gabilans to the east, the foreboding Santa Lucias westward, and nearby the Salinas River whose waters filled his boyhood swimming holes a few miles north. It's reasonable to suppose that he visited *his* river often — the fascinating wrong-way watercourse that differed from most American rivers by flowing north instead of south, eventually winding through many of his future pages. Unquestionably, he responded to the river's tug upon him by exploring the riverbank tunnels formed by overhanging willows and sycamore branches. Memories of all this — plus sights, sounds, and smells of the big Willoughby ranch — would come welling up to furnish the background for *Of Mice and Men*, published in 1937. (In the movie version, the big ranch is given as Ranch No. 3, near Soledad.)

Steinbeck left the ranch as unexpectedly as he had left Stanford. When next heard of he was in Salinas, swallowing his pride, for a reunion with his family. Life was soon back to normal, with John "home from Stanford for a while." But for John there was one slight difference — he was now writing most of the time. Even when out rabbit hunting with his old friend Glenn Graves, he would flop down near the Salinas River to scribble a few lines.

The few times he avoided pen and ink were on drinking parties out in the Alisal. He and his old high school pals swapped reminiscences and raised more than one toast to Takashi Kato, who had departed with his family for God knows where. And the liquor they consumed was the cheapest they could come by.

At the only dance he attended, the girls agreed they were unimpressed. They described him as awkward, conceited, and a teller of off-color stories. Several claimed he pulled a pouch from his pocket to offer them marijuana, with which he experimented briefly.

Almost daily during this period he took long walks out of town, curiously wearing a long, loose-fitting overcoat and muffler, no matter how hot the day. Ranchers driving along and spotting ahead what looked like a scarecrow in swishing garments knew that when they drew abreast they would recognize the Steinbeck boy — and they did. John's favorite route was along the Old Stage Road, the Gabilans his eastern backdrop, while westward spread fields of sugar beets and beans, their shoots pushing through the loam to form vast seas of green. A few little patches of lettuce were also on the way, experimental crops that followed the lead of a Pajaro rancher (and that one day would become a lure for the dust-bowl refugees from Oklahoma). When observed on the old road, John appeared oblivious to everything, his head bowed in thought, face running sweat, and overcoat flapping. Motorist Eddie Johnson, of high school days, would occasionally offer him a ride back to town, but John always waved him on.

Soon, however, John and Eddie did travel together on the narrow-gauge from Salinas out to Spreckels where both worked, John as a bench chemist from June until December of 1922. Meanwhile, on November 11 of that year, after second thoughts about higher education, John applied for readmission to Stanford, reporting his employment at the sugar mill and providing letters of reference. He was reaccepted at the university.

CHAPTER EIGHT

IN the journalism building on registration day of January 1923, Steinbeck spotted Dook Sheffield and suggested that they room together in Dook's basement digs in Encina Hall, Room 32. He would remain there until Dook's graduation in June. It was the beginning of their long friendship.

At once there was mutual respect between the pair. Steinbeck found Dook almost painfully modest, always eager to please, and completely unselfish. Since they were both majoring in English, they had much in common. Dook was seven months older than John, somewhat shorter, spoke with precise diction, and wore his brown hair slicked down and parted in the middle, collegiate style.

The dismal little room shared with Dook inspired John to decorate. It wasn't long before he showed up with a roll of wallpaper, with which the two decorators papered the room waist high, breaking the monotony of bare walls. One eyesore in their Encina room that irritated them both was a wooden packing box atop a steamer trunk. What could they do with such an ugly encumbrance? Was there no way to disguise it? John chided himself at being baffled. After all, hadn't he come from a long line of inventors? Eventually he came up with a plan. He brought in a roll of Turkey-red broadcloth, explaining that they would mask the damned monstrosity. When they finished draping the grotesque pile, hiding it completely, they discovered that John's idea had worked; they had created a unique stepped dais. To give the two-tiered platform added distinction, they extended more broadcloth out over it in a graceful canopy held up by almost invisible wires. On the top step of their altar they placed a foot-high Kewpie doll, modestly cloaked in a white silk handkerchief. John named her the Goddess of Chastity.

On turning off the electric lights, they were delighted to find that a can of Sterno placed on the lower step burned with an eerie, greenish flicker. Their next move was inevitable. When they expected visitors, they would light the spectral flame. And the callers, on entering, would behold an astonishing sight: the room's occupants on their knees in the wavering gloom, facing the shrine, hands upraised, bodies swaying. The only sound would be the mumbling of incantations to their goddess. John was pleased with his inventiveness and pleased, too, at putting chastity where he said it belonged — in a plaster of Paris figurine.

One evening early in the term John brought out a little sheaf of manuscripts, some of them written on the Chualar ranch, and stated without qualifications or embarrassment:

"I'm going to be a writer."

No mention this time of "journalism." His mind was made up. And he mumbled something about not wanting to be second best. Secretly skeptical, Dook studied his new roommate silently. No pointed comment came from Dook, in fact, until 1962 when, a million Steinbeck words later and half a world away in Stockholm, in a scene stirring with flags and trumpet calls, King Gustav VI presented the Nobel Prize to Steinbeck. Both before and after the brilliant ceremony, of course, messages poured in from readers around the world. Dook's was first — and the most moving of all. From California he wrote: "I suppose it really was almost forty years ago that a guy moved in with me and told me, 'I want to be the best writer in the world.' I believed him and while the reputations of Shakespeare and some others are probably safe for the present, it's been a pretty good try and I've been cheering on the sidelines all the way. . . ."

But in that dingy basement room of Encina, when the young man from Salinas announced his ambition, all that Dook could manage after a while was to blurt out that he, too, hoped to write. As he spoke, John impatiently fluttered the pages of his manuscripts, then hesitantly asked if his companion would like to hear a few of his stories. Politely Dook agreed to listen.

"Some of the stories he read to me seemed to be pretty fair," Dook recalled, "though most of them were certainly not polished work. What fascinated me most was his method of reading them, for he seemed to be struggling between self-consciousness and emotion over what he had written. His voice went higher than normal for him and he read rapidly, with words quickly pronounced but tending to blur at the ends, as if he were embarrassed at uttering them. His tone in general was flat, but it was the flatness of carefully restrained excitement.

"He kept good control of his face while reading, except for one eyebrow, which arched high as he reached something he liked, or that moved him, or that he was dubious about. He was inclined to hurry, particularly at the end of sentences, underemphasizing the final word or two and rushing into the next one as if afraid of being interrupted. When he finished, he never looked at his auditor, but grimaced deprecatingly, the single eyebrow as high as it would go, and his hands fumbling busily at arranging the sheets and putting them away while he made some off-hand comment about the piece he had been reading or, as often as not, abruptly changing the subject."

By this time, John knew that only one thing in the world mattered to him — a literary career. He would be a writer or nothing! An author or a bum! To hell with Stanford's basic requirements that would get him a degree!

He promptly announced to the startled authorities that he did not want a degree. He did not want courses that could not aid him in his life's work. He would take only classes that appealed to him. While the administration disapproved, he was permitted to attend school under those terms, or perhaps on the condition that he would complete the requirements at a later day. One absolute stipulation, however, was that curricular choices must first always receive the English counselor's approval.

During the first three quarters of 1923, he took courses in composition, versification, oral debate, English classics, Roman civilization, history of Rome, general zoology, elementary French, and more military science. Additionally, he showed interest in biology, marine life, and sociology.

Occasionally, after signing up for a course, he would be disappointed with the subject or the professor and drop out. He frequently avoided final examinations. A few of the professors went along with his arguments that the course was his sole interest and that passable grades didn't matter except to keep him in college. Why, he wanted to know, should he be forced to write down answers when they weren't an accurate index of what he had learned? His pleas apparently were heeded to some extent during his years of sporadic attendance.

As the school year wore on, John and Dook often argued late into the night on every conceivable subject, two of the most popular predictably being sex and bootleggers. Dook was impressed by John's frequent references to one or another phase of nature. He confessed his love for storms, the sound of thunder, drumming of rain, fog swirling in. He loved dogs and always had had one or more of them.

John's dislike for dances and social gatherings soon became apparent, not that it hampered his efforts at becoming acquainted with

(above)
The mid-Victorian home in
Salinas where
John Steinbeck was born
February 27, 1902.

Dorothy Hight Vera

(below)
The young Steinbeck proudly
rode Jill, The Red Pony, in
the Salinas rodeo parade of 1913.
Here he is at parade's end.

Glenn Graves (left) and John on a rabbit hunt near Salinas.
The dog was the first he named Omar (full name, Omar Ki-Yi).

(right)
Max Wagner poses outside
his home in Mexico.
Shortly afterward, when
he moved to Salinas,
he became one of John's
close boyhood friends.

(below)
Metal filings got in John's
eyes at the Spreckels
factory, but that didn't
keep him away from dogs.

(above)
Shirtless and well-greased,
George Mors and John Steinbeck
await the opening gun
in the old Freshman-Sophomore
Tie-Up at Stanford.

(right)
George L. Mors, John's
first Stanford roommate

(right)
Carlton A. (Dook) Sheffield,
John's Stanford roommate
for two semesters and
a lifelong friend

(below)
Briefly at home from
Stanford, John stops on
the Salinas river bottom
to scribble a few lines.
Glenn Graves is with him.

Frank Fenton, Stanford
crony, on whom John
tried out many of his
early writing efforts

One of the few
pictures taken of
John during his
Stanford days

(above)
The Brigham home at
Lake Tahoe, where an
overload of snow
crashed through the roof

(right)
The caretaker's
cottage near the
Brigham mansion,
where John wrote
The Cup of Gold –
and cooked pots of
sumptuous beans."

(right)
"Strong Man"
Lloyd Shebley
pretends to
hold up tons
of rock

(below)
The Tahoe Hatchery,
where John and
Lloyd Shebley took
care of the
fingerling trout

members of the opposite sex — and making the most of it! His strong urges in that direction had continued unabated ever since his parents had trustingly left the one-legged hired girl in their home.

A testimony to his prowess was the time Dook introduced him to a coed whom Dook regarded with frustration as an unassailable citadel of virtue. Since she had repulsed his every advance, he felt certain that even John would get exactly nowhere. A stone woman!

Several nights later, John exhibited a small aluminum box of Merry Widows — three rolled-up condoms much in demand — and announced he was going on his first date with the paragon of purity. "Might as well leave those rubbers behind," Dook laughed. "They'll do you no good."

Late that night John returned home and, while he was sleeping, Dook peeked into the little aluminum box. Only one rubber remained!

"Why, the bastard!" Dook exclaimed in envy.

There was also the evening of John's amorous tryst with a Palo Alto girl on a hillside behind the campus. Their *couche d'amour* was gently sloping. Locked in each other's arms and oblivious to the effects of gravity, they rolled from the top of the hill to the bottom, engaging in their intimacies all the way. It was no mean feat. During a subsequent literary discussion with Steinbeck and several others, the well-read young lady casually referred to Henry James's *The Turn of the Screw* as a real triumph. Only John knew what she really meant.

In the spring of 1923 Dook spent the Easter holidays at the Steinbeck home in Salinas. When they returned to school they were caught up in classwork and spent much time talking, studying, reading, and writing, a routine interrupted only by John's night walks. These jaunts took place frequently and were always unplanned. John would leave the room silently and be gone for hours, returning most often with an air of deep abstraction. Immediately he would busy himself with pen and paper without speaking, as if conversation would shatter his mood or interfere with the setting down of ideas which he had formulated while away. Dook found it wise not to speak to him at such times. If John answered at all, it was with grunts and monosyllables. He could be far from gracious. The night rambles became an almost sure sign to Dook that John was working out some story idea.

Included in his Stanford output, written either then or later, was a satire titled "Fingers of Cloud," the story of a subnormal girl who deserted her Filipino husband because he wouldn't quit storing horses' heads in the fire barrel. In this story appears the first Steinbeck bunkhouse, anticipating by fourteen years the sharply drawn ranch-hand quarters in *Of Mice and Men*. The student effort: ". . . Burlap tacked loosely on the walls, a littered floor of dust-colored wood, a few boxes to sit on, and the fat-bellied stove, that was the lounging room of the bunkhouse. Three of the pock-marked brown men played cards on the floor under a coal oil lamp. . . . Ten or twelve more of the squatty figures were dumped about the room, half smiling because there would be no work in the beet fields the next day. . . ." *(The Stanford Spectator*, February 1924.) His second and last story to appear in the *Spectator* (June 1924) was "Adventures in Arcademy," a satirical allegory of Stanford life, with meanings sometimes hidden almost too well. At one point, however, the story clearly makes reference to President Ray Lyman Wilbur and his valuable but wearisome reminders not to mix alcohol and gasoline:

"A short distance farther, on the shell road, I came upon a large group of people in appropriate costumes who worked busily over beakers and test tubes and flasks. From far off a Voice was heard, wailing:

" 'Gasoline and alcohol will not mix,' and then despairingly, 'Gasoline and alcohol must not mix.' There was much grandeur in the last, which goaded the workers to greater efforts with their bottles. Before long, however, the Voice spoke of other more dignified and professional matters."

John also wrote three poems for the *Stanford Lit*, all of them comic satires: "If Eddie Guest Had Written the Book of Job: Happy Birthday" and "If John A. Weaver Had Written Keats' Sonnet in the American Language: On Looking at a New Book by Harold Bell Wright," plus "Atropos: A Study of a Very Feminine Obituary Editor."

While the Stanford walkways and other physical features of the campus appealed to John, some of the student customs did not. One that he found especially objectionable was the caste system, the practice of setting some students apart because of their parents' social position, wealth, political influence, and the like. There were cliques within cliques. Nearly all fraternities and sororities operated on this basis, and John with his hatred for snobbery, felt it unfair. To him, there was something wrong about labeling certain people superior or inferior to others.

Dook was a member of the Los Arcos eating club, which had individual tables in semi-private rooms in the Stanford Union, and on several occasions John was his guest there. Although John knew a number of the members and tried to be courteous to the others as well, a stand-offish attitude was apparent among them. They mistook his politeness and reserve for aloofness. What he did find hard to hide, though, was resentment over the pretensions of some members, especially a small group who sat together, spoke partially in French, and poked fun at the table behavior of others. It came as no surprise to Dook Sheffield that John turned down his overtures to join the club. "It's probably just as well he wasn't interested." Dook admits, "for after he had been a guest at the club a few times, one of the guys told me that if he were put up for membership, he'd have been blackballed." Not that it would have bothered John. Some tramps he knew had better manners, he said.

His own manners were impeccable — when he wanted them to be. And that was always the case when he visited his favorite bootlegger in San Francisco, Madame Torelli, whose speakeasy was an upstairs apartment at Greenwich and Powell streets.

She was a refined, elderly Italian woman with white hair and an elegant wardrobe about twenty years out of date. A visit to her place was like a social call in which all the proprieties must be strictly observed. She tolerated no vulgarities; no raised voices, and no boisterous activities.

Madame Torelli preferred, too, that her guests be properly attired. Her favorable attitude toward John may have been based on his first visit when, for some reason or other, he was wearing a dinner jacket and on his best behavior. He was an instant success and continued to be, even when he subsequently appeared in mere street clothes.

Madame Torelli had a wide line of liquors, but on absinthe she placed an absolute limit of two half-ounce glasses per evening. Once John talked her into parting with an entire fifth of absinthe, but she exacted a solemn promise that it was to be drunk only a very little at a time, and he kept his word. When it was gone, though, he felt under no further obligation.

On one occasion, absinthe had dire consequences, but not Madame Torelli's brand. That had long since been used up. The trouble followed a ribald weekend during which he and Dook had gone their separate ways, John carousing in some nearby town, Dook in San Francisco. When the weekend was over, the two got together in their Encina room with horrendous hangovers, both solemnly swearing off booze forever.

At the precise moment they were taking the pledge, Carl Wilhelmson, another student writer, came in, saw their condition, silently put a pint of Canadian Club whisky on the table, and just as silently withdrew. They eyed the pint for a few seconds without speaking.

"Come to think of it," John then said, "it was gin I swore off drinking. I could use a pickup right now."

"Me too," Dook said.

Dook stopped with only a few drinks, but for John it was just the beginning. After finishing the pint, he left the room for an hour or so but returned with some Chinese absinthe, for he knew his sources. Although Dook took only a few sips of the yellowish-green liquid before lying down, John still drank with gusto.

About eight o'clock John left to keep a date with a girl. Dook went to sleep but woke up toward morning with a sense of suffocation. His roommate was bent over him and leaning heavily on his chest — drunker than Dook had ever seen him. He was cradling a bottle in his arms and crooning to it while tears ran down his cheeks.

Dook made him get off his ribs, but his roommate's crying grew worse. Steinbeck was blubbering about his girl, whom he had taken for a walk around the lake, and insisted that she was a "wonaful baby." She had told him her life story, he said, and it was very, very sad, and they both wept. Then he had told *his* sad life story, and they wept some more. He couldn't stop his tears even now.

John refused to go to an all-night diner on the highway, so Dook, who was feeling worse than ever, went alone. Next day John skipped classes, but not his partner. When Dook returned from classes late in the afternoon, he found John lying on the bed, fully dressed and half facing him, his eyes staring. Save for some milk and sandwiches from the little cigar store down the hall, he had eaten nothing all this time.

Dook, sitting down at the table to study, could feel John's eyes on him. Time and again he made some remark, but John never answered. Finally Dook said, "Okay, if you want to be a boor, to hell with you." And he left to get a bottle of pop, returning in about fifteen minutes.

John hadn't changed his position and didn't move as Dook resumed his seat. Again Dook spoke, but still no answer. Experiencing his first twinges of apprehension, Dook went to the cot and grasped John by the shoulder. It felt like iron, as did his arms and legs. They wouldn't bend.

Thoroughly alarmed, Dook tried to shake his roommate, which was like trying to shake a log. After a few minutes, just as Dook was wondering what doctor to call, the rigidity went out of John's muscles and he began to breathe deeply. For a little while he lay there silently, and then in a barely audible voice he said, "That was close."

Eventually he explained that the attack had come on him suddenly as he watched Dook study. Since he couldn't speak or move, he had tried to convey the call for help with his eyes, but Dook hadn't understood. The pain of his stiffened muscles was agonizing. When Dook left the room, John said he was convinced he was going to die. He could have, too, though he had no history of earlier attacks.

Neither of them knew the exact cause of the muscular catalepsy, but of course blamed it on the consumption of assorted liquor. Thereafter, they took it easy when sampling absinthe, which they viewed with extreme distrust — especially the Chinese variety.

In June of 1923, after taking selected examinations, John invited Dook to visit him in Pacific Grove on the Monterey Peninsula, where both he and his sister, Mary, would be attending the summer session of Hopkins Marine Station, an adjunct of Stanford. Dook happily agreed to come after graduation ceremonies at Stanford.

When grades were announced, John found that he had made not one A but three of them — in versification, elementary French, and Roman civilization. He had failed nothing and received no grade lower than C-.

John and Mary were alone in the family's Pacific Grove summer cottage when Dook finally showed up on his way home to southern California. They greeted him with cheers, demanded to see his bright new diploma, brewed him coffee, and begged him to stay "a long time"; their parents would be remaining in Salinas awhile. Showing Dook through the tiny house, John assigned him to its one bedroom, explaining that he and Mary would sleep on cots on the vine-shielded porch.

Dook had never seen John looking happier. Steinbeck loved the place and said so. Small as it was, the toylike house overflowed with pleasant memories for him — memories, surely, of summer vacations spent there as a boy, of getting lost with his pony, of wading in the surf nearby, of gathering wild blackberries with his mother.

Attending the general zoology class at the Hopkins Marine Station took only part of John's and Mary's time. While they were in class, Dook did the housekeeping and much of the cooking, although eating for the most part was highly informal. In the mornings the first one up ground coffee beans in a large, old-time grinder and brewed the coffee in a granite pot that held at least half a gallon — seldom enough on days with no classes. Sometimes there was mush and eggs, and always toast, on which almost anything would be smeared (John liked his with lemon juice squeezed on it). Time permitting, the coffee drinking stretched well through the morning and followed the family pattern of years — everyone drank it while seated on the wooden curb bordering the narrow street out front, feet in the gutter. But on a number of occasions, especially on mornings following wine bouts, there was time only for Dook to rush his wards to school by auto.

A Salinas girl named Phyllis, who had a nearby cottage and was also a student at the marine station, sometimes ate at the Steinbeck house. The foursome danced and sang, went fishing or crabbing, and picnicked at Point Lobos and up in the Carmel Valley several miles away. John occasionally went walking alone after dark and sometimes took Dook with him. They explored the shadowy parts of Pacific Grove, Monterey, Carmel, and the pine forests. When they weren't talking books, they moved along silently thoughtful.

John's zoology class instructor suggested one day that students bring in toads for dissection. John volunteered to get them and per-suaded Dook to help. When the two set out that evening to round up the hoppers, they were joined by five or six others armed with flashlights and gunnysacks. John was the guide. On the outskirts of Pacific Grove, just as he had predicted, they came upon their quarry. Toads were everywhere, skirmishing in the street, noisy in the gutters. Their songs tattered the night. The hunters snapped on their flashlights, and the concert stopped.

Some of the toads melted away like greenbacks in Frisco. But others, hypnotized by the glare, surrendered to reaching hands. A few cooperative ones even plopped into the sacks of their own accord. An hour or two later the huntsmen toted their dripping bags to a cottage. They had toads by the hundreds. But what to do with them till morning? Someone found an answer by emptying a dresser and filling its five drawers with their slippery charges, thereby turning the once dignified old bureau into a makeshift prison that squeaked, rumbled, and thumped all night long.

Next morning the triumphant students lugged the entire dresser through the marine station to the laboratory, dribbling toads all the way. The professor, having hoped for a dozen or so specimens at most, was so overwhelmed and dismayed that, like the prince in the fairy tale, he turned into something of a frog himself, hopping madly around after escapees and croaking out orders to remove and release the whole slimy lot. Even so, John glowed at having led such a bountiful safari. The episode resulted in the memorable frog hunt in *Cannery Row*.

With summer school ending, John and Mary sadly bid farewell to Dook, who left for his home in Long Beach. John's own plans were nebulous, but he knew this much: he would skip the autumn semester at Stanford and work again at the Spreckels sugar mill in Salinas.

CHAPTER NINE

THE large laboratory on the southwest corner of the sugar mill's second floor was a popular showplace, complex and mysterious. Around the walls ran a waist-high bench, and spaced along it were shirt-sleeved young men doing strange things with beakers and vials, test tubes, thermometers, and pipettes. They were the bench chemists, each assigned a different duty. It took many skills to run the biggest sugar mill on earth, and here an important, though relatively simple, task was performed — the checking of factory samples, step by step, for density, purity, sugar content, and the like. Every few hours foremen studied the findings to head off sugar wastage.

For John, the Spreckels laboratory was ideal — a home close to home and a fine place to earn a steady salary again as a bench chemist. He was on the night shift in the laboratory and knew the mill intimately, knew the shortcuts, the dodges, the hideouts, and knew to the second how long he'd have before the next samples arrived. On the end of his bench he kept some tools of his own — a writing pad and pencils. And in his free periods he would jot down notes to himself or dash off letters to Dook. Little could distract him, for he had grown accustomed to the factory's noisy heartbeat of bells, code calls, whistles, and the noisy exhaust of steam. Even the rumble of beets going into the great bins and the nearby fierce grinding of machinery went unheard. The giant plant was a good teacher of concentration.

However, John did not spend all of his free time writing, nor did he cater to the supervisors. He much preferred the company of Mexicans who had been on the hot presses or those who had left the steaming "hog pen" down below, where the beet pulp fell after being sapped of its sweetness. The shirtless, booted hog-pen gang knew what work really was, and so did the Mexicans of the factory yard. In free hours John listened to their grievances and, when asked for it, gave advice, for laboratory men were held in high regard.

To him, the Mexicans' crudely told stories were often gems. At least two of their tales — the story of old man Ravanno and the story of the ex-corporal — went into *Tortilla Flat*. Another incident that amused him, but which he didn't use, although he recounted it in a note to Dook, came from hunchbacked Pablo Ortiz. Pablo was not a handsome fellow and had no sweetheart, but he did have urges that took him to The Row on California Street every payday. On these exursions he carried a few lemons. And always before love-making he insisted on performing one simple rite to determine whether his impatient hostess was free of disease. Politely he would ask permission to apply a little juice of the lemon to an intimate anatomical region — "Jus' the littlest squeeze, *señorita.*" If the application made his partner wince, Pablo backed away. More than once he thought the lemon had warned him just in time.

At first the girls were tolerant of the ritual, but not after a while. When he would knock at the front door, they would peek out, and, if he carried his little bag of lemons, refuse to let him in.

Hereafter, Pablo sadly told John, he would go to a different house. What he wanted to know now from the laboratory one was this: Was the lemon test dependable?

John bowed his head in pretended reflection. "No, Pablo," he said soberly after some time. "It isn't. Not lemons! Never lemons! Instead, *mi amigo,* use *oranges!"*

The little hunchback thanked him profusely. Before letting him go, however, John thought some more and voiced a revised opinion — there was really no test both fast and reliable; to be absolutely safe, alas, Pablo had better stay pure.

On registering at Stanford early in January of 1924, John took a single-occupancy room on the fifth floor of Encina. The cubicle was severly plain but its dormer window, facing north, looked out upon a pleasant setting of trees and grass where sheep sometimes grazed. His self-styled monk's cell was much to his liking, for time was moving on and he had charted heavy seas for himself. Solitude would be welcome. He must write, write, write! Why, next month he would be twenty-two!

In all ways Steinbeck was noticably maturing, his writing becoming sharper. More of his shyness was melting. He was making friends. His sense of humor, although still lusty, was taking on subtlety. And his sympathies were more pronounced than ever.

Although in previous years he had listed English as his major, he now changed it to "Journalism option in English," a technicality. Although he had not forsaken the idea of writing fiction, it seemed expedient to have news writing in reserve. After consulting his adviser, as required, he signed up for the long-awaited course in short-story writing, together with courses in Greek tragedies, history of the Great War (1914), history of philosophy, news writing, three military courses, and polo.

As in former years he patiently explained to each professor that he was entering the course only to get certain information that might be offered. Thus he would either find what he sought or he wouldn't, and no examination could have any real bearing. Some of the faculty allowed him to have his way, apparently convinced through personal association that the lessons would not be lost on him.

Deliberately John bunched his classes in the forenoon, leaving most of the afternoons wide open. On finishing his last class for the day, he usually went directly to his room, spread out books, paper, pens and pencils, and set to work. Studies out of the way, he would start writing. His output that semester was tremendous — verse, short stories, satirical sketches, and notes for future work. Some nights were reserved for playing and drinking. Occasionally John would get together with his sister Mary, now also enrolled as a student. Their special bond of affection never wavered, and whenever the two thought they were being overheard, they happily reverted to their secret *Morte d' Arthur* talk.

When fatigue began to show in his afternoon writing, he would take a breather, usually between four and five o'clock. Lighting a fresh cigarette, he'd stroll down the hallway to Room 563 and hammer on the door. Invariably the lone occupant would groan and invite him in. The room was that of Frank Fenton. Like John's, Fenton's desk was heaped with books.

The ambitious Fenton had his heart set on becoming a college professor — an ambition that would eventually lead him to the acting presidency of San Francisco State College. John's commotion at the door would find him just settling down to study.

"Because of John's visits," Fenton says, "I nearly flunked Anglo-Saxon. Well, John would flop in the spare chair, cross his long legs, blow smoke through his massive nose, casually wave his hand, and say, 'Go on and study. Don't let me bother you.' For a while I'd try to study, but with him sitting there, I could feel his eyes upon me and finally had to give up. 'Well, for God's sake,' I'd say, 'let's have it!' "

John would open the visit with some trivial comment and gradually work his way into stories of ghosts or leprechauns. Fenton recalls the tale of a blue leprechaun who flung a ham on the floor, and the story was told so vividly Fenton almost believed it. When challenged, John insisted that leprechauns and elves were very real. Sometimes John revealed the germ of a plot by talking of Sir Henry Morgan, the buccaneer, who, of course, would become the leading character in *Cup of Gold*. Often the two discussed King Arthur and his knights.

One afternoon John brought in a sheaf of manuscript — the delightful story of an uninhibited *señorita* and her vacuum cleaner, an episode he had heard somewhere. Since Fenton was associate editor of the *Stanford Spectator*, John wondered if he would like to run the piece. Fenton read it and was fascinated. However, living by rules, he submitted it for approval to Dean George Culver and Chaplain David Gardner, who, finding it unsuitable for undergraduates, turned it down. Protests were of no avail. How interesting it would be to compare that early account of Sweets Ramirez and her sweeping machine with the final version in *Tortilla Flat!*

"In all my life," says Fenton, "I've never known anyone else to concentrate so deeply on writing or work so hard at writing as John. But writing was an instinct with him, like breathing. From John's own lips, I learned that he enjoyed the very act of writing, of wiggling a pencil along to form words, even if only making out a laundry list. Funny guy."

During this period at Stanford John boasted about his scholastic independence. Several times he signed up for a course that looked promising, but when he found it dull or disappointing after a few sessions, he substituted something else. Once, having entered an English class given by Vandyke-bearded Professor Seward, he attended faithfully until the course was more than half finished, but then one of the professor's jokes suddenly had a familiar ring. Checking back over his records, he claimed that he had taken the same course a year earlier and earned a high grade.

He became better acquainted with Margery Bailey who taught eighteenth-century English literature although their friendship was an explosive one with frequent feuds and periods of hostility. He never found himself able to fit comfortably into her little coterie of males, so that social relations, when they did exist, resembled an armistice. Although with a face of almost majestic beauty, Miss Bailey had thick ankles and legs and a temper. One day, on entering her office John found her seated behind her desk with a bowl of narcissus at her elbow. Her delicate pastel dress fell in flowing lines, disguising her boxcar build, and a long jade necklace added further softness. Even her pulled-back hair, knotted into a bun in back, was in keeping with the faintly Oriental tone of the whole scene. The caller was enthralled. He blurted:

"Why, Miss Bailey, you're beautiful!"

Miss Bailey looked up, startled, apparently interpreting his compliment as a taunt. Her face flushed with anger.

"You damned impertinent puppy!" she blurted. "Get out!"

Miss Bailey followed Steinbeck's later successes with much interest, and at the time of his death she told the press that, while she had not liked John's "cynical work" in the Stanford literary magazines, she considered his stories about the Salinas Valley and its people "pure, beautiful, sound and masculine."

One professor who won his admiration and became a personal friend was Harold Chapman Brown, who taught history of philosophy. Tall and tanned, blue eyes glowing in a round face, he was well liked by most students. John applauded his independent attitude toward the university. Professor Brown wouldn't conduct early morning classes "when no one can think" and refused to teach more than four days a week, which might interfere with his tennis. Walking restlessly up and down before his class, he traced the development of philosophical theories from the early Greek period, and through it all, would inject his own witty views. Brown's abhorrence for war left a deep impression on John, so much so that the professor's ideas may have found their way into future tales, notably *The Moon is Down*.

Among the strong influences upon him was Edith Ronald Mirrielees, from whom he took the short-story writing course and gained a great deal in art and technique. She was a taller woman than average, bespectacled, her dark hair streaked with grey. Among her suggestions to would-be writers was that they carry pocket notebooks in which to jot down descriptions, character traits, bits of arresting conversation, unfamiliar words, and other reference material, something which Steinbeck later astoundingly denied doing. "I rarely make notes," he said, "and if I do I either lose them or can't read them" — a statement contrary to the evidence. He not only took copious notes on researching *East of Eden*, but for numerous other works.

Edith Mirrielees was probably one of the first to spot Steinbeck's latent talent. Their association continued for many years, during which she criticized a number of his novel manuscripts before they went to the publishers, and he valued her criticism. In one of her classes he is believed to have submitted the short story, "A Lady in Infra-Red," which was the germ of his soon-to-be-written *Cup of Gold.*

Whether or not John was a formal member of the English Club, then a dynamic literary force on campus, is uncertain, but he attended many of the meetings and associated closely with several of the active members of the group, including Margery Bailey. John's iconoclastic views frequently put him in the limelight at these meetings — and not always favorably. Few surpassed him in sarcasm and irony. When the conversation strayed from literary subjects, for instance, he might argue on behalf of a generally disliked campus political candidate, throw a few barbs at some Biblical contention with which he disagreed, or run down the campus caste system, intimating that the English Club itself might be tinged a bit with that taint. As the debate crackled on, Miss Bailey would become visibly distressed and try to guide the talk into calmer channels. Her announced "time for tea" occasionally worked.

Often after an English Club meeting Steinbeck would take a campus stroll with one of the members, Webster (Toby) Street, who was interested in playwriting. They became such good friends that John served as best man at Toby's wedding in Palo Alto. Sometimes the two would discuss one of John's story plots. More than once they touched upon the flicker of an idea Toby had for a three-act play — an idea he would put into written form in 1926 under the title of *The Green Lady.* However, its finished form left him unhappy — he couldn't make the second act work — and in a future day he gave the idea outright to his old friend. After a trip with Toby into Mendocino County to see the play's forest locale and its character types, John would one day rewrite it into a novel *(To a God Unknown).*

Most social events, though popular with others, were usually disparaged by sophisticates of the English Club. One was the formal junior prom, the very thought of which irritated Steinbeck. He attended only one. In speaking of it, he sometimes colored details to match his mood, but in the main his accounts were consistent.

Only the "best people" attended this stylish ball. Young blades debated whom to invite. Fathers spent lavishly on gowns for their daughters. For weeks ahead of time, socialites and social climbers buzzed about one topic — the forthcoming junior prom.

John and his friend Montgomery Winn, a future attorney in Honolulu, decided to go — but in their own way! As a sign of protest toward the caste system they invited Chinese twin sisters from San Francisco. A week before the big night, John's sister Mary, a prominent Alpha Phi who had never seen the girls and knew nothing of their nationality or background, tried to be helpful. The young ladies, she told John, might use her sorority's facilities for last-minute primping for the dance if they wished.

On the night of the prom John and Monty accompanied their dates from San Francisco to Palo Alto on the train, planning taxi conveyance out to the campus. But they hadn't reckoned properly. Every cab in town had been reserved for days, some for weeks! While Monty remained with the twins at the station, John darted out to round up transportation of any kind; even bicycles would do. Luck dealt him an ace. He returned with a Chinese laundry wagon — an ancient and battered Model-T-Ford, with doors in the rear. But it ran. And it managed to make its rusty, rattling way to the campus without mishap.

Luxurious limousines lined the driveways of every fraternity and sorority that the tired old vehicle passed, each house striving to outdo its neighbors. Cadillacs and Packards were commonplace — though some were borrowed — while lesser autos were shunted into the shadows. A gleaming Pierce-Arrow or two gave a desired air of haughtiness.

Eventually the laundry wagon was within a block of the Alpha Phi porch, where distinguished visiting alumni mingled with young couples, all about to depart for the prom. Nearer and nearer crept the rattletrap, as though bent on delivering bundles of wash before collapsing on some scrap heap. The clatter increased. John could see the sorority sisters watching in horror as the motorized eyesore swerved into their driveway and clanked to a stop.

Sqeezing himself from behind the wheel, Steinbeck skipped around to the rear of the truck and swung open the doors. Out jumped Monty, who gallantly handed down the twins. Clad in full Oriental dress, only a trifle self-conscious, the Chinese girls smiled and waved demurely at the staring people on the porch. Leaving the delivery wagon right where it drooped, the young men picked up the girls' dressing cases and escorted them into the house to search out John's almost apoplectic sister. (It was weeks before she forgave him.)

But at the ball the Chinese girls were the hit of the evening, and their partners were deluged with requests for dances with them. Even the chaperones began to thaw. All considered, the young men's not-too-subtle strike at campus hypocrisy paid off — and, in the process, Steinbeck for once had a fine time at a big party.

Who the girls were, or where the boys had met them, remained a mystery, although it was rumored they were prostitutes.

For the most part, John conducted his social life off campus. Among the few coeds he dated was a popular and attractive girl, Harriet (not her real name), who had more than an academic interest in life. On weekends, the two would take off for a round of passionate love-making in such catch-as-can hideaways as the countryside afforded. On one memorable occasion she announced that her aunt would soon be away from her remote Santa Cruz beach home for a week. Maybe she could get a week's leave, if John would care to join her there.

He would.

Ensconced in the empty house, the pair headed almost immediately for the bedroom. At the conclusion of their love-making Harriet began rummaging through her suitcase. "O, where is it? Where is it?" Somehow she had forgotten to bring her douche equipment. Frantically, and without success, the two searched the house for a substitute.

From the bathroom John called, "Hey, let's try this."

Harriet came running. John stood beside the medicine cabinet and held out a yellow tube of toothpaste — Forhan's, by name. Better than nothing, he explained. Tomorrow they'd buy contraceptives in town, but time was too precious now. So the toothpaste was tried, applied with a toothbrush handle, probably the first time in history that a tube of Forhan's was used for such a purpose.

More and more, as that year of 1924 rushed along, John thought of attempting a book, encouraged by Edith Mirrielees. She would point out flaws in his work and praise good points, be sternly critical, then restore his ego. Always, at interview's end, gently and quietly, she would fire him with hope.

In grades for the two quarters that year, he had again done well, earning an A in the short-story course and Bs and Cs in all others, save military. Dook Sheffield met John in Pacific Grove during the summer where both wrote for a while and where John fell under the spell of Jeffrey Farnol. When not scribbling, they read so much Farnol they started talking in the synthetic dialect of the author's picaresque characters.

Unable to find work on the Monterey Peninsula, they took jobs in Manteca at the Spreckels branch factory in that sizzling interior town. After a month, they were glad to escape to cool San Francisco, where they dated girls, visited whore houses, consumed oceans of Prohibition liquor, and went stony broke. John decided to take another leave from Stanford for the autumn semester and went to Dook's home in Long

Beach, where they were both determined to resume serious writing and make a fortune. Dozens of stories went out, new and old. But back they came, so fast that John thought them intercepted halfway to New York and turned around. Desperate for money, they tried door-to-door selling of radio receivers. Their only sale was to Dook's elderly aunt. Then a bonanza! They contracted to address, stuff, and mail Christmas seals, three quarters of a million of them. For weeks they toiled, but finished the unglamorous job and were paid.

Before leaving alone for the north, John turned over to Dook a fat manila envelope. It was stuffed with rejection slips and bore this scrawled summing up: "The Literary Adventures of Dook and Me."

CHAPTER TEN

BACK again at Stanford for the beginning of the school year in 1925, John almost ran into trouble with Dr. William Dinsmore Briggs, chairman of the English Department. Vividly Frank Fenton recalls the day Steinbeck entered the chairman's office to get his proposed courses of study approved. Vividly he recalls the character behind the desk — an authority on classical literature, master of many languages, and a devoted academician every inch. Dr. Briggs looked like a schoolteacher right out of Dickens. A retiring man of precise diction, he wore impeccable clothes of English cut, although his high stiff collar was much too roomy to be stylish. From his rimless glasses, clipped to his nose, plunged a swooping silk ribbon anchored to his lapel. But of particular fascination was his bald head that settled low in his collar when he was seated and deep in thought, a trait that kept strangers on edge; they wondered if, like a turtle, he would ever pull in his head all the way.

Over the years Dr. Briggs had developed a soft spot for students fond of literature or showing any promise of writing. A lucky thing for Steinbeck, since his adviser could be a stern taskmaster. Adjusting his glasses, the counselor bent over his caller's list of courses and carefully checked them off, one by one.

"Elementary Greek — affirmed," Dr. Briggs intoned, ticking off the items. "Essay writing — affirmed. Pre-Med dissec —" He looked up, stretching out his neck. "Mr. Steinbeck, what is *this?*" A formidable pause. "I don't think a medical course in dissection will be permitted. After all, you're an English major."

"Yes, I know the rules," John said, "but I think 'Dissection' will accept me, sir, if you consent."

"But cutting up cadavers!"

John sucked in his breath, started to argue, caught himself. "I want this course very much."

"Why?"

"Well, I want to know more about people. This could be one way."

Slowly Dr. Briggs' head sank back into his collar. He sat there silently for some time, removed his pince-nez, and polished it. When his celebrated head popped up again, his grey eyes twinkled. "I think you have a sensible idea, young man," he said. "I approve." And when the great teacher bowed Steinbeck out of the office that day, he was smiling like a prospector who had spotted a glint of gold. That one brief meeting keynoted much of the caller's Stanford career and the years that followed. Curiosity about people never left him.

Whether Steinbeck ever took "Dissection of the Human Body," or how long he remained in the course, is unknown, for the university fails to list him as a student in it. Still, to Fenton, sitting in on the episode, John's talk with his adviser pointed up the young writer's unorthodox approach to his studies, and why, after a rather extended career at Stanford, he remained the despair of so many faculty members.

"Dissection" notwithstanding, Steinbeck did take courses that semester in elementary Greek, essay writing, the feature article, European thought and culture, and two courses in military science.

But uppermost in his mind must have been the beckoning, nagging "A Lady in Infra-Red." For her sake, he would even cut down on bottle parties and dating. And, to avoid any possible distractions, he moved into a one-room shack at the rear of a big house beside Francisquito Creek in Palo Alto. It promised privacy and the rent was cheap.

The room was barely seven feet square and crowded with a steel cot with springs, a table, and a rickety chair. To draw water, he dealt with a faucet outside his door; for toilet facilities he went to the big house. Cooking was done in the yard on a small open-air grill balanced on some rocks. The cubicle was formed from what might have been an old woodshed or part of an abandoned stable.

Privacy? Solitude? A dream! Almost at once John's popularity boomed. His college friends were delighted with the place and praised him for his discrimination. Nightly, as many as six or seven buddies would wedge themselves inside for bull sessions and beer drinking.

On one occasion they got all choked up discussing plans to buy a commemorative brass plate for the door; they wanted the world to know the bug hutch as a shrine when John reached his literary immortality. Deeply moved, John said he felt like weeping over their concern but instead demanded to know when they were going to get the hell out; he had work to do. Finally he was driven to limiting visiting hours to Friday nights.

But even this failed to stretch his time, for down the street, only a block away, was the irresistible home of E.C.A. Smith, where the English Club met on occasion. Despite the masculine name, E.C.A. Smith was a small, vivacious, hip-swinging divorcee, ash blonde and blue-eyed, and the astounding part was that John wasn't attracted by her feminine qualities. Knowing John's inclinations, his friends could scarcely believe it. But what drew him into the company of E.C.A. Smith was the simple fact that she was a successful writer!

Since she wrote of masculine subjects in a masculine style, and male authors were preferred, she used her initials in place of "Elizabeth" and sometimes took the *nom de plume* of John Breck or John Barton. In addition to writing two columns daily for the Associated Newspapers, she sold short stories to leading national magazines. Her name had been triple-starred for outstanding excellence in Edward J. O'Brien's collection of *Best Short Stories of 1921*.

Like Edith Mirrielees, E.C.A. Smith saw a bright future for John Steinbeck and couldn't do enough for him, even to sacrificing time needed for her own work. By the hour they talked stories and style or relaxed over checkers, for which John showed little aptitude. Usually his wide shoulders were draped with his grandmother's fringed biddy shawl, his favorite garment at this time.

When he let it be known that he hoped to stretch "A Lady in Infra Red" into a book, she urged him not to delay. Every morning, shortly after daybreak, he would start work with pen and ink at the table in his tiny shack. Right then he was establishing a habit that would stay with him for years — using a fine-pointed pen on the unused pages of old ledgers, whose smoothness and feel he liked. His script was dainty small. Early each morning, in response to a knock, he would look outside his door and find on the stoop a steaming pot of coffee sent by his proud mentor. Delivery was made by Polly, "E.C.A.'s" seventeen-year-old daughter. Moreover, when John's manuscript was well along, Polly typed it for him.

The course in European thought and culture, taught by Professor Edward Maslin Hulme, was the academic highlight of the year. The tall professor had jowls that gave him the look of a basset hound. His voice, when lecturing, would rise and fall until he sounded on the verge of song.

John was amused when the teacher, an outspoken agnostic, touched upon cannonization. One account involved Simeon Stylites, who worshipfully stood atop a pillar for seven years, pointing heavenward and sustained only by faith and donations of food. When finally back on the ground, poor Simeon couldn't lower his arm, but the plight paid him the dividend of sainthood. Another example, and the one John liked best, concerned Mary of Egypt, a former actress and courtesan. To atone for her sins, she headed for Jerusalem to worship. Coming to a river, she was unable to pay ferry charges across, but the ferryman impiously offered to ferry her over in exchange for her newly acquired virtue. Mary agreed. And because she so willingly sacrificed her "jewel of great price" for a cause so glorious, Hulme concluded, she too was sainted.

Sometimes after class the students on their own reviewed ancient hagiography and read corollary material. One unrelated account that appealed to them was the fiction by Anatole France about the nearsighted priest who rejoicingly baptized a flock of penguins which he mistook for people. So great were these varied influences that the students made a game of choosing the most unlikely candidates imaginable for sainthood. John chose a pig, a mean thief of a pig who was turned from her sinful ways into channels of righteousness and a worker of miraculous cures. The story, written in school probably for the pleasure it gave him, showed Steinbeck's early versatility in selection of subject matter, style, and presentation. It isn't known what changes were made in the manuscript prior to the eventual publication of St. Katy the Virgin, but Fenton vaguely recalls that the original was in verse form.

("In the chapel at M — there is a gold-bound, jeweled reliquary, and inside, on a bed of crimson satin repose the bones of the Saint. . . . This holy relic has been found to cure female troubles and ringworm." — St. Katy the Virgin.)

John's leisure moments were becoming more infrequent, save for Friday nights when his campus friends would descend on his tiny room. When his mind wasn't on his studies, it was on his novel. He was even neglecting his platonic relationship with E.C.A. Already he had written innumerable short stories without a single sale. When would the tide start turning? Little did he dream of the discouragements ahead.

It was inevitable that his long, hard drive would slow down. Finally he reached a mental block. Had his austerity program been too austere? Checkers only bored him. Long walks failed to help. A friend deduced that pent-up sexual desire might be his problem — or that some mental shock might end the doldrums.

Then it happened — a disquieting, though welcome interlude that worked. A rejoicing Steinbeck recounted it at a subsequent Friday-night beer blast, disguising names, and why he never wrote of it can only be guessed. The telling was enriched by his mumbled drolleries, ever-rising voice, grimaces, and that expressive arching of an eyebrow.

One Saturday afternoon, on a strictly "no visitors" day when he was wearing a disreputable robe, he glanced from the window and was horrified to see a billowy matron picking her way across the back yard toward his shack — Mrs. Emmerson Garfield, a well-to-do temperance leader from a nearby town for whom he had once worked. She was pious, persnickety, a gossip, and her daughter was engaged to his good friend Walter Fairs. Fortunately someone from the big house stopped her to chat, delaying her progress.

John's eyes swept the small room in alarm. Scattered clothes were everywhere, along with empty beer bottles, two overflowing ashtrays, and curvaceous, dark-haired Suzanne, an old San Francisco flame who had apparently managed to bypass visiting regulations. She wore a transparent negligee and stockings, nothing more. John fought off panic. No use pretending he wasn't home; it would be just like his landlord to bring the caller inside.

With lightning moves he hauled up the cot's covers and hustled Suzanne, as well as other incriminating evidence, under the cot. He was trying to smooth his curly brown hair when the knock came. He caught his breath and opened the door.

On entering, Mrs. Garfield parted her pursed lips to observe that the room was no bigger than a thimble, but she complimented him on good housekeeping. He choked on a "thank you." The visitor came quickly to the point. Having obtained his address from Walter Fairs, she was stopping by for two reasons. She wanted to offer John employment at her home next summer and also wanted his opinion of her daughter's fiancé. Was his friend Walter a worthy young man? A churchgoer? "Knowing your family so well, I can ask you these questions because your own standards are so high." John weakly admitted this was so.

The caller settled heavily onto the cot as she rattled on, and John took the flimsy chair. He was thankful for this, since from his vantage point the scantily clad girl under the cot sprang into view. Tightly sandwiched between the dusty floor and the sagging springs, Suzanne was lying face down, head turned in his direction. Her lips were con-torted. She was pressing her nose in an obvious effort to hold back a sneeze. And her pleading dark eyes looked straight into his. He turned away.

In answer to interminable questions from Mrs. Garfield, John launched into some compelling fiction on the saintly qualities of Walter Fairs and so warmed to his subject that he convinced even himself, he maintained later, that Walt was the soul of rectitude, save when staggering around speakeasies. Now and then he stole a glance at Suzanne. And died each time. He realized that if the room's secrets were known, Walt's very association with him would damn his pal forever — and end job offers as well.

Mrs. Garfield stayed and stayed. Several times she half-rose as if to go but dropped back again, springs squeaking. After nearly an hour, she thanked John for his help, gathered her skirts, and got all the way to her feet.

"All's clear," John piped when she'd gone.

There was a movement under the cot. And out from beneath it squirmed Suzanne, her face damp with perspiration, hair bedraggled, negligee streaked with cobwebs and dust.

"I thought that bitch'd never go!" she gasped, letting fly with a long pent-up "Achoo!" Tenderly she rubbed her bottom. "And it's all your fault, John Steinbeck."

With the arrival of June 1925, John started winding up his university affairs. Had it really been five years since he had stepped from the streetcar onto the Stanford campus for the first time, hungering for knowledge that would help him become a successful writer? Where had the time gone?

While others would be receiving their sheepskins, he would be slipping away empty-handed. What to do next? There was New York City, publishing center of the world, luring nearly all the world's top-flight writers and would-be writers. But by now he knew how great were the odds against his ever crashing the literary world in a big way. And there was less promising California. Whatever his thoughts for the future, looking back over his five broken years at Stanford, he must have realized he'd been a non-conformist all the way. He had taken nearly forty courses and had amassed ninety-three units, giving him, roughly, junior standing.

A clue to Steinbeck's feelings about the time spent at Stanford and at high school, as well as the teachers who influenced him, may be found in a revealing article he wrote in 1945 for the *California Teachers Association Journal*. It begins with a simulated conversation with his young son, pointing out how difficult the formal learning process would

be and adding that "adults forget how hard and dull and long school is."
"Learning by memory all the basic things one must know is the most
incredible effort. Learning to read is probably the most difficult and
revolutionary thing that happens to the human brain, and if you don't
believe that, watch an illiterate adult try to do it. School is not easy, and
it is not for the most part very much fun, but then, if you are very lucky,
you may find a teacher. Three real teachers in a lifetime is the very best
of luck. My first was a science and math teacher in the high school
[Emma F. Hawkins], my second was a professor of creative writing at
Stanford [Edith Mirrielees], and the third was my partner and friend,
Ed Ricketts [a marine biologist who operated a laboratory on Cannery
Row in Monterey]."

His comment on Emma Hawkins: "She aroused us to shouting,
book-waving discussions. She had the noisiest class in school and she
didn't even seem to know it. We could never stick to the subject,
geometry or the chanted recitation of the memorized phyla. Our speculation ranged the world. She breathed curiosity into us so that we
brought the facts or truths shielded in our hands like captured fireflies.

"She was fired and perhaps rightly so, for failing to teach the
fundamentals. Such things must be learned. But she left a passion in us
for the pure knowable world, and me she inflamed with a curiosity which
has never left me. I could not do simple arithmetic, but through her I
sensed that abstract mathematics was very like music. When she was
removed, a sadness came over us but the light did not go out. She left
her signature on us, the literature of the teacher who writes on minds. I
have had many teachers who told me soon-forgotten facts, but only three
who created in me a new thing, a new attitude and a new hunger. I
suppose that to a large extent I am the unsigned manuscript of that high
school teacher. What deathless power lies in the hands of such a person!" — (C.T.A. Journal and Out West.)

Unfortunately Steinbeck failed to leave a written appraisal of Edith
Mirrielees, the single teacher at Stanford who possessed, for him, that
"deathless power"! One memorable Stanford teacher in five years —
just one! By Steinbeck's clear implication, that single imaginative and
creative instructor had made his entire university career worthwhile.

John Steinbeck, on a sunny day in June, said goodbye to a few
friends and faculty members, gathered together his possessions, not
overlooking his first draft of what would become Cup of Gold, his pen,
and his grandmother's biddy shawl, and moved along, his university
days at an end for good.

CHAPTER ELEVEN

IN San Francisco, with the mournful sounds of foghorns faintly reaching him, John shoved his heavily revised manuscript from under the shielded, low-hanging bulb and spoke aloud to the empty room:

"The hell with it!"

"A Lady in Infra-Red" was still a stubborn problem. It was six months since he had left Stanford, filled with his bright dreams — six months divided between Salinas, Pacific Grove, and the Bay City. Yet now, a half-year later, he was beset with serious doubts about his swashbuckling tale of adventure and romance. Could it be that he wasn't ready for a novel?

"The hell with it!"

Right then he gave in to a temptation that had long been nagging at him. Maybe, he thought, he could do better in New York with short stories. The next day he inquired about travel fares. Thanks to help from home, he booked passage on a freighter leaving later from a southern California port; he would board her there, but, first wanted to visit Dook. On a November day of 1925, the rusty, red-and-black freighter *Katrina* made ready to pull out from Wilmington, California, for New York. John stood at the rail looking down at Dook below. The two tried shouting to each other, but words were swallowed up in the rattle of chains and hoists and the noisy skirmishing of stevedores. Gestures proved meaningless. At last, in the wake of a tug, the old Luckenbach ship started inching away from the dock. As it did, Dook traced three words on the door of the warehouse behind him — *ave atque vale*. John nodded, understanding.

Not long after the *Katrina*'s departure, John began writing regularly to Dook, shipboard notes that revealed interest in all he saw. His early letters described the ship itself, later told of his tourist-class companions, pictured the changing shoreline of Lower California, noted the progressive differences in visible marine life, and paid tribute to certain fish and birds that followed the wallowing tub for days.

In the squalid sections of Panama City, John concentrated on heavy tippling with like-minded travelers and a few natives. And he was pleased that many of the sights there confirmed imaginary scenes for his stubborn story about "A Lady in Infra-Red," but he made it plain that more work on it would simply have to wait — a decision that he was obviously trying to justify, if only to himself.

In Havana he met a pretty girl — a very pretty girl and *expensive* — and the one hundred dollars he had taken along for a start in New York dwindled steadily. It took money, he found, to buy rum drinks, take carriage rides, and otherwise live in the worldly manner. He had his first qualms on glimpsing snowy New York through a porthole. All that remained of his initial capital was three dollars — a figure he subsequently reported in a newpaper article, though in a letter to Dook he set the sum at five cents. ("I crept ashore — frightened and cold and with a touch of panic in my stomach. This Dick Whittington didn't even have a cat." — *The New York Times Magazine*, Feb. 1, 1953.)

Fortunately John's sister, Elizabeth, was in New York, living with her husband in a comfortable but cramped apartment consisting of one large room, a tiny bathroom, and a screened alcove. Thanks to his brother-in-law, who lent him thirty dollars, John slept in a hotel the first night. Next day he took a room three flights up in Fort Greene Place in Brooklyn, and, through arrangements made by his brother-in-law, went to work as a laborer in Madison Square Garden, then under construction. Since he was young, big, and husky, he got the muscle-punishing job of pushing 150-pound barrows of cement, endlessly — ten to eighteen hours a day when he wanted overtime pay of two dollars an hour. Other men in the line of barrow-pushers, mostly blacks, sang and joked as they labored, but not John. He felt his back would snap, his arms yank out. And once long ago, he recalled, he had considered the Big Sur highway job a tough one!

At day's end came the pitching sidewalks, meaningless cry of news vendors, subway roar, pounding temples, numb climb up three flights to a dingy room with green walls, and nightly snacks of beef stew and "coffee and sinkers in a coffeepot." Then dully back with his agony of bones to more barrow-pushing. He never forgot the experience, though he did forget how long it lasted. Maybe a month. Maybe six weeks.

Nor did he forget the workman who missed his footing and fell from a scaffold near the ceiling, landing in a splash of bloody jelly beside him.

97

John became violently ill on that occasion.

When the job finally ended, Tex Rickard, sports promoter, congratulated the workmen on their dedicated service. The public would be grateful; it was a blessing indeed. Now the six-day bicycle races could start on time.

John was out of work but briefly. His uncle, Joe Hamilton, who owned a prosperous advertising agency in Chicago and had connections, came to town and spent lavishly. (". . . [Uncle Joe] stayed in a suite in the Commodore, ordered drinks or coffee and sandwiches sent up any time he wanted, sent telegrams even if they weren't important." — *The New York Times Magazine.*) The uncle lost little time landing John a $25-a-week reporter's job on the *New York American*. For a month young Steinbeck did general assignment work for Mr. Hearst — and hated every minute of it. He couldn't wheedle stories from bereaved people without becoming emotionally involved himself and was a rank failure at swiping photographs from the piano top. Further, he couldn't help coloring facts with fancy and suffered torture when his stories underwent blue-penciling or were callously tossed to rewrite men. Frequently he clashed with his superiors about these matters, about his assignments, and even about Hearst policies. Undoubtedly he would have been fired on the spot save for his uncle's influence. Instead, he was transferred to the federal courts in the old Park Row office — a job for seasoned hands, not new men. Even so, the old-timers there, outwardly cold but inwardly warm-hearted, tipped off the newcomer to story sources, tried to teach him the nuances of pinochle in the press room, and covered for him when he was away. He never forgot their help. "You can't buy that sort of thing," he said. While on the *American*, he spent most of his free hours on fiction.

At that time John was living in the old Parkwood Hotel on Grammercy Place — in a small, $7-a-week room, six flights up, turn left, grope. Although his parents sent him what little money they could, his funds were always low. However, he managed to establish wavering credit in a cheap, wide-open but inconspicuous speakeasy in Greenwich Village, where he became acquainted with Ducky, the handyman. He liked Ducky. Not many people did.

Ducky was stooped, withered, and beaten, his head almost hairless. He scratched a lot. The ancient roustabout received no wages, but worked in return for a little rent-free room in back. Also, he was allowed to keep any small change he found on the floor when sweeping out. He was always on call and ran errands. But the biggest boon of all for him was "Ducky's Special," a gallon jug of miscellaneous liquors given to him weekly. He would take the jug to his little back room and tie on a good one.

Ducky's drinks were indeed special — and specially concocted. A gallon jug, topped with a funnel, stood behind the bar, below and just out of sight of the patrons. When an imbiber left part of his drink, it went into the jug, And it didn't matter what these dregs might be — whiskey, gin, wine, beer, sweet drinks, and sour, everything. All were dumped into the funnel and became a part of the strange and wonderful libation that was passed along to Ducky, seemingly just before it might explode and wreck the building.

Early one Sunday morning before business hours, Ducky was swabbing floors when a stately woman in furs climbed from a taxi and rattled the street door. The taxi waited. Ducky scratched and tried to wave her away. She wouldn't go. Finally Ducky let her in. A close look told him that on the previous night she must have hung on a beaut. Her plump cheeks quivered, hands shook. Her eyes were bloodshot.

Haughtily she demanded an eye-opener. Ducky refused, explaining that he was not permitted to touch the bar stock. Then, an inspiration.

"Well," he said softly, "maybe I could part with a shot of 'Ducky's Special' — for a dollar. Good stuff. Very rare."

"By all means," the caller agreed. No questions. She wanted something in a hurry.

Ducky brought the jug from the back room, secretly marveling at his inspiration. He poured her a shot-glass of the shadowy liquid, which she downed at a swallow, nearly strangling. Then, slowly, as the tears left her eyes, she settled back on her stool, and a great peace came over her.

She paid with a silver dollar, which Ducky pocketed, and demanded a refill. Ducky obliged, accepting another coin. By the time the woman reeled into the street to fall into her cab, Ducky's pockets were jingling.

When John heard the story, he filed it in his mind for possible future use — and eventually did incorporate it into *Cannery Row*. (It was in that story, at La Ida, that Eddie accumulated booze in much the same way it had been done for Ducky.) And once at the Greenwich Village bar — just once — John Steinbeck bravely tried a slug of "Ducky's Special" himself — on credit.

Life in New York began to look a little brighter when John became

99

acquainted with a dazzling showgirl. He first spotted her one morning as he shaved at his window. She was in the window of a neighboring building, clad in a dressing robe as she prettied herself for the day. Thereafter, either chance or design put them in their windows at the same time, and soon they began waving at each other. Before long, they were meeting on the street.

Mary Ardath had a $100-a-week walk-around job in the Greenwich Village Follies, and deserved to be there. She was a peach parfait. John would wait for her at the stage door and they would eat together at small hideaway restaurants, Mary usually taking the tab. Her always-broke boyfriend didn't mind this generosity, however, for he thought himself in love. She begged him to quit the *American* and writing and get into advertising. He refused, and Mary Ardath ran away to marry a midwestern banker. The farewell note she left for John was shattering.

Two days after the love affair crashed, John was fired from the *American*. And this time there was no Uncle Joe around to help.

John began writing short stories more furiously than ever. Nothing sold. Unable to find another newspaper job and reluctant to tell his sister of his financial plight, he became what he called a "journalistic freelance" and occasionally unloaded news stories to various papers — shaky way to make a living. One feature story in which he took pride was based on his discovery of Kid McCoy, the former pugilist, wearing a blue smock and tending the quotations board in a big bond office — a story that made the wire services. John soon gave up all forms of journalism, however, for his income would not meet even simple living expenses.

Among the people he knew in those uncertain days was Mahlon Blaine, a stimulating companion and bold illustrator, who liked John and did what he could for his threadbare friend, introducing him to some publishers and a few writers.

Still no results. Doggedly John kept on with his fiction, mostly short stories with a metropolitan background. Dook, who would eventually see them, describes them as pretty good, "in spite of a tendency toward restrained sentimentality."

Skimpy meals, or no meals at all, were having their effect. John became jumpy and irritable. Blaine lent him a dollar. He invested in two loaves of rye bread and some dried herring and holed up in his room for a week. ("I was afraid to go out on the street — actually afraid of traffic — the noise. Afraid of the landlord and afraid of people." — *The New York Times Magazine.*)

At the suggestion of Blaine, he sent a batch of his stories to Robert

M. McBride & Co., book publishers, and was surprised to be summoned to their office. Guy Holt, then editor of the firm, proved outgoing and friendly, okaying most of John's tales, suggesting some revisions, and saying that if John would turn out a half-dozen more pieces of like quality, McBride's might put them in a book.

With new hope, John kept writing, existing on the slimmest food rations possible. Occasionally friends supplemented his meager diet, but he still didn't get enough to eat. He wrote and rewrote, discarded and polished and reviewed. Finally he finished the requested work.

Bundling his stories together, he set out for the publishers. In the McBride building he walked down the hallway to Holt's old office. There he paused. The name of the man he sought was not on the door; in its place was the name of another. He felt vaguely uneasy.

Inside, in an anteroom, he inquired as to the whereabouts of Mr. Holt. The friendly receptionist said that Mr. Holt was no longer with the company but had joined the John Day publishing firm. Stiffly John followed the girl into the sanctum of the new editor, dropping his precious packet upon the man's desk.

The new editor, who seemed to John overburdened with his own importance, riffled through the manuscript, scarcely glancing at the pages while announcing that McBride's policies had changed. The company was at last "going places," and second-rate stuff was no longer being purchased. Steinbeck's submissions fell short; they simply did not meet the required literary standards.

According to John's own account, as later related to Dook Sheffield, he heard the new editor's blunt verdict, and a time bomb exploded within him, possibly because of his repeated setbacks and built-up tensions. At any rate, scarcely aware of his actions, he leaned over the desk, raged at the man, cursed, and shook his fist. Ejected from the building — or so he informed Dook — he collapsed on the sidewalk a few blocks away and was taken to Bellevue Hospital, where he was treated for shock and malnutrition.

This version of the affair is frankly doubted by his sister, Elizabeth, who points out that John often embellished the truth for the sake of a better story. Further, since she was living in New York at the time of the alleged incident, she feels she would have been notified had her brother been hospitalized. Sharing her skepticism are Elizabeth Otis, of McIntosh and Otis, Steinbeck's agents for many years, and Elaine Steinbeck, the author's wife for nearly two decades.

In any event, no book was published. Later John presumably looked up Holt and found him unable or unwilling to make any fresh commitments for the publishing company he had joined. However, Holt did offer to introduce Steinbeck to James Branch Cabell, who was in town, but John refused, saying that although he admired Mr. Cabell's work tremendously, he didn't want to risk disillusionment. Holt reported this to Cabell, who sent a handwritten note to his young admirer. It read:

Dear Mr. Steinbeck: Sometimes I too wish I did not know the undersigned. — James Branch Cabell.

Fed up with the hostility of the big city, suddenly filled with "unadulterated fear" of it, and plain homesick, John poured out his miseries to a college friend in town. The friend lined up a job for him on another Luckenbach ship, San Francisco-bound. ("And he didn't have to urge me, either. The city had beaten the pants off me." — *The New York Times Magazine.*)

The trip back home restored his health and a measure of his confidence. On the way he scoured fittings, fought a bully, shot craps, and made close friends with some crewmen. He arrived in San Francisco about the middle of July, 1926.

Immediately he headed for Palo Alto where Dook was doing postgraduate work. When his old friend emerged from a classroom, there stood John, looking a bit worn but grinning as of old. Dook took him home to meet his new wife, Maryon, and put him up at their cottage. John stayed two weeks, talking volumes, but Dook could tell the old restlessness was upon him. Then one day Steinbeck shoved off without explanation.

CHAPTER **TWELVE**

nEAR the southwestern end of Fallen Leaf Lake is Fallen Leaf Lodge, 6,321 feet up in the High Sierra. The rocky slopes of Mount Tallac, sprinkled with pines, rise steeply behind the huddle of toy buildings.

On a summer day in 1926, Toby Street casually answered the office telephone, and on the other end of the humming country line was John Steinbeck, visiting somewhere at nearby Lake Tahoe. The two old friends talked a long time. Hopefully, Toby asked if John wouldn't like a job at the lodge. John hesitated. Toby sketched the setup, explaining that he was there from Stanford with his wife and child, working as well as vacationing, and that his mother-in-law, Mrs. Price, owner of the place, could use more help. Then his bait. Foxily he added that, in addition to other duties, John would be required to drive the mail stage daily — a 16-cylinder Pierce-Arrow! That did it. Cars, like dogs, were irresistible to John. He accepted at once.

Only three miles long and with an average width of less than a mile, Fallen Leaf Lake was tiny compared to mighty Tahoe, but the winding road along its shore carried him five miles before Mrs. Price's resort slid into view.

John made a dependable workman, putting in long hours and doing the roughest sort of labor, but he liked the job, liked the people around him, liked the country. His work was varied. Sometimes he hauled rock and gravel, helped with construction, erected rock walls, and built stone dams on Glen Alpine Creek. One chore John never objected to was driving the Pierce. Behind its great bank of throbbing cylinders, he made good but careful time on the daily six-and-a-half mile run into Camp Richardson on Lake Tahoe for the mail and arriving guests.

For relaxation on days off, he went hiking up Mount Tallac and enjoyed encounters with occasional Washoe Indians, whose customs were a constant fascination. He made notes on their superstititions, traditions, and dependence on primitive cures, which sometimes, beyond all understanding, seemed to work. Out of this experience came his story of the young Indian named Jimmy in *America and the Americans*. Once in a while an incident involving the Washoes struck the sardonic chord within him.

There was the time he gave a lift to a squaw named Katie, who had started out on foot for Lake Tahoe. He and Toby sat up front in his Model-T sedan. Their passenger climbed into the back seat, which ". . . had a high ceiling and was designed to look like a small drawing room." — *Holiday*, July 1954. When she was settled in the tonneau, tools were handed in, crowding her, but she made no complaint. On the journey the sedan overturned, trapping the squaw inside. Luckily no one was hurt. Shouting to the woman to remain calm, the two men left on the run to get crowbars. On their return, the squaw was gone! A jagged hole in the roof explained her escape route. Apparently Katie had found an axe among the tools and had chopped her way out. Steinbeck grimly observed that one never knew what a Washoe would do.

One day John saw an old Indian gathering willows to weave into baskets. His skin was loose and wrinkled. His bony fingers flew. By way of conversation, John asked his age.

"Me don' know," said the patriarch, not pausing in his work. "Pretty old."

"How many children you got?"

"Me don' know. All boys."

"Well, how old is the oldest?"

"Me don' know," said the ancient Washoe, screwing up his seamed face in thought. "But him older'n me."

Through Mrs. Price, Steinbeck became acquainted at the Camp Richardson post office and general store with Mrs. Alice Brigham, the wealthy widow of a noted San Francisco surgeon. She invited John to visit at her summer home, just a mile and a half north on the lake front, where she was vacationing with her daughter, son-in-law, and two grandchildren. John was captivated by the house, with its immense living room, booklined walls, grand piano, and great stone fireplace. When Mrs. Brigham one day asked him if he would like the job of caretaker after the family left, including use of a cabin all to himself, he eagerly accepted.

In the meantime, he continued on at Fallen Leaf, as did Toby, who had decided to skip the autumn quarter at Stanford. When cold weather set in, the two friends decided to leave together for the coast, Toby to register for the university's winter quarter, John planning a brief visit to San Francisco before taking on the caretaking job for Mrs. Brigham.

Just before daybreak, shivering in their overcoats and blankets, they shoved off in John's open-air, patched-up Model-T. The old car sputtered, and Toby cursed it softly.

"Don't worry," John said. "She'll make it easy."

Their troubles started almost at once, adding considerably to John's old-car knowledge. By the time they reached Truckee, the radiator was boiling. At an untended service station they found a solidly frozen, stretched-out water hose, which, when lifted, stood out straight as a bowsprit. The car's problem, and theirs, was solved at an all-night gas station and short-order house.

Soon they found that when both of them were in the car, steep hills were unclimbable. Lizzie tried hard, groaning and shaking, but just couldn't cut it. John did some pondering. Innocently, he suggested that Toby get out and push while he himself remained in the driver's seat to work the pedals — logical strategy, he pointed out, since he owned the car and knew her whims. Although the chore would be mighty monotonous, he explained with a straight face, he'd willingly endure it. As things wound up, they took turns shoving and eventually their back-breaking efforts put them on Donner Summit.

Going downhill, travel was easier, but now a mysterious chunk-chunk-chunk came from under the car, up front. Neither man could diagnose this new ailment, but they were afraid to stop. On the outskirts of Sacramento, the noise swelled to a pitch of agony.

John pulled off the road. They climbed out and stared in disbelief— *almost all the front-wheel spokes were gone.* One by one, all the way from Donner, they had been tearing out and flying away, like slats from a raided henhouse.

Then and there Toby reached a decision: "Joy ride's over — I'm taking the bus."

And he did. To this day, he doesn't know how John ever reached San Francisco.

When John returned to Mrs. Brigham's now deserted Tahoe estate after several weeks on the coast, he came outfitted like a sourdough off to the Yukon and armed with house keys which had previously been given him. The job was made to order, and he looked forward to a long stay. His duties were primarily to watch over the place, but his biggest immediate task was putting up storm shutters against the approaching winter and looking after his own needs. He sawed and split plenty of wood for the cast-iron cooking and heating stove in his cabin, a snug one-room cottage of stone a hundred yards from the empty Brigham home. He arranged the cabin furniture to his liking and laid out writing tools, typewriter included.

Having brought along numerous early drafts of "A Lady in Infra-Red," he gave the story considerable study in his cabin, made a few more abortive stabs at revision, then decided not to push it. In due time, he knew, a fresh outpouring of words would come, but the time was not yet ripe. That he was working on some story, however, is indicated by a letter he sent to Toby Street, in which John asked for a small dictionary, one book lacking in the Brigham home — ". . . apparently the Brighams are so perfect in their mother tongue that they do not need one. . . I do." He also said he would send Toby "some manuscripts" pretty soon (which he did not do). Much of his time that first winter was spent on correspondence, reading, getting the feel of the place, and conquering fear — fear of being alone and fear of the dark. In a letter to Toby he expressed these feelings: "[the fear] comes on me at night mostly, in little waves of panic that constrict something in my stomach. . . ." And, "I wanted to break that fear in the middle, because I am afraid much of my existence is going to be alone, and I might as well go into training for it."

As he had done at Fallen Leaf, he made regular trips to the Camp Richardson post office, a mile and a half south, but in this off-season period the boat with mail from Tahoe City came only twice a week.

The snows arrived early, mantling the pines and closing nearly all roads. Only rarely, however, was he blocked in his trips for the mail. Usually he trudged along the very edge of the beach, where the lake's wavelets melted the flakes as fast as they fell. Or he would make the trip a few yards farther inland on skis or snowshoes. Sometimes he pulled a toboggan along when he expected to return with purchases from the general store.

One day in February 1927, as he stood on the Richardson pier, he gave a hand to a black-haired young man of about his own size and build who was struggling off the boat with a bedding roll and and bulging suitcase. Instinctively John liked Lloyd Shebley, who worked for the Fish and Game Department and had come to open the Tallac trout hatchery on nearby Taylor Creek.

Thereafter, whenever returning from Richardson, John would stop at the hatchery to open and read his mail, chat with Shebley, and warm up over coffee. The two became fast friends, sharing a concern for nature and conservation and a deep love for this snowy country. Soon they were eating at each other's place. In John's cabin the menu was always a big pot of beans with bits of bacon rind, simmered together all the preceding night. Neither ever tired of what John called "magnificent beans," a specialty of his house.

One package John could count on receiving every week was a dozen carefully padded eggs from his mother. (In a letter to Toby, John asked that his parents be reassured of his well-being and for God's sake not to be so fussy — "Be as honest as you can, but picture me in a land flowing with ham and eggs, and one wherein woolen underdrawers grow on the fur trees. Tell them that I am living on the inside of a fiery furnace, or something.") Other parcels from home arrived around February 27, his twenty-fifth birthday.

The mail also brought about the same time an item of more than passing interest — an advance copy of the March 1927 issue of a new magazine, *The Smokers Companion*. It contained a short story written by John Steinbeck under the pseudonym of John Stern — his very first sale. The story was "The Gifts of Iban," "a charming fantasy."

"Vol I, No. 1" of the short-lived *The Smokers Companion* was an illustrated, twenty-five cent periodical intended as "a national magazine for hearth and home." According to the editor, Gerry Fitzgerald, Steinbeck had insisted upon the pen name because he disliked the name of the magazine and did not want to be linked with it.

"The Gifts of Iban" is set in a forested region inhabited by "crawlers," "web-spinners," and other creatures. Iban, maker of songs, offers gold and silver and himself to his sweetheart, Cantha, who is likened to a dragonfly. His gifts are the golden shafts of sunlight through the trees and moonbeams silvering the underside of leaves. The lovers spend the night together. Next morning, when discovered, they marry to avoid disgrace. Neighbors nonetheless shun Cantha. In a short while, with her mind now poisoned against Iban by her mother, who declares his gifts valueless, Cantha leaves him.

Considerable evidence indicates the tale may have been written during John's Stanford days, or shortly thereafter, as it is strongly reminiscent of "Adventures in Arcademy." Phraseology and word combinations are similar, and both fantasies reveal a fascination with colors. A prized copy of the magazine, probably the only one extant, is kept under lock and key in the Arents Collections at the New York Public Library. Curator Perry Hugh O'Neil, who knew Steinbeck, says the author received about fifteen dollars for his story.

In late March or April, John briefly left the Brigham estate for a temporary job at the Tallac hatchery, a job arranged by Shebley. For a week or two he did miscellaneous chores and then spent full time getting the Brigham house and grounds ready for the family's return.

Mrs. Brigham and her housekeeper were the first to arrive, followed during the summer by Mrs. Brigham's daughter and son-in-law, Mr. and Mrs. Harold Ebright, and their two sons, Charles, nine, and Harold, Jr., seven.

During the first few weeks of their stay John was occupied with many duties, but before long he settled into a routine largely of his own making. The family took little of his time. They were now treating him as one of their own, but John missed Lloyd Shebley, who had moved from the Tallac hatchery to the larger trout hatchery near Tahoe City at the far end of the lake.

More and more Steinbeck's mind turned to "A Lady in Infra-Red," which he was now calling *The Cup of Gold*, and, to get it moving again, he would wander away alone to think things through. Borrowing a mug or one of the china cups from the big house, he would fill it with coffee in his cabin and tote it to one or another nearby glade, where he would sit on a log and ponder the plotted circumstances surrounding Sir Henry Morgan and the mysterious woman known as *La Santa Roja*, or the Red Saint, whose beauty drove men mad.

It was a productive period — for him if not for Mrs. Brigham. So absorbed did he become in replotting that he often neglected to return her chinaware, and for nearly forty years thereafter her descendants would occasionally come across missing cups buried in drifted pine needles or wedged in rotting wood.

The family lingered at Lake Tahoe into the early fall, and John took over as tutor for Mrs. Brigham's grandchildren. He was a stern taskmaster and saw that his charges studied their arithmetic, geography, and spelling. "It's nice to think we had a future Nobel winner as a baby sitter," Harold Ebright likes to say. In the evenings the family would gather in front of the fireplace, and with the wind moaning in the chimney, John would go into an old routine. He told ghost stories.

John's second autumn and winter there found him going full tilt on his novel. Alone again and with few distractions, he kept his pen working long hours in his cabin, often to music from a small phonograph. His favorite record was Dvorak's "New World" Symphony, which seemed to him to parallel the story of the Welsh boy who ran away to the Indies to make his fortune and never did return to the home for which he yearned. "The book follows the symphony," Steinbeck said, going on to explain that he had carefully regulated the pace of the book's action, the tonal quality of the narrative, and the word sounds to conform to the major changes in tempo and mood of the music.

Although he became fairly well adjusted to the fierce winds and night sounds, John admitted that his fright continued. In a letter to Toby he said not to tell anybody but that whenever he heard an unusual noise at night he was afraid to go outside to see what it was. Otherwise, he liked his "watchman's" job.

But his main concern that winter remained *Cup of Gold*. At last he stabbed its closing page with a final period. It was finished, this time forever.

And he didn't like it!

On February 25, 1928, he wrote to Dook in utter dejection. His remoteness from home and being alone as another birthday neared didn't help. Like the novel itself, his letter showed the influence of Cabell and Byrnes, with overtones of Farnol:

". . . I finished my novel and let it stand for awhile, then read it over. And it was no good. The disappointment of that was bound to have some devastating though probably momentary effect. You see, I thought it was going to be good. Even to the last page, I thought it was going to be good. And it is not. . . .

"I have a new novel preparing, but preparing very slowly. I am not quick about such things. They must roll about in my mind for an age before they can be written. I think it will take me two years to write a full length novel, counting the periods when I walk the streets and try to comb up courage enough to blow out my brains. Isn't it a shame, Duke, that a thing which has as many indubitably fine things in it as my Cup of Gold, should be, as a whole, utterly worthless. It is a sorrowful matter to me.

"As usual I have made a mess of this letter. I didn't finish it the other night. Now it is late the night before the boat, and I shall get very little written on it. Do you realize that I am twenty-six now. I don't. I don't feel twenty-six, and I don't look that old, and I have done nothing to justify my years. What a shame. Yet I don't regret the years. I have enjoyed them after a fashion. My sufferings have not been great nor have my pleasures been violent. . . .

"I am finishing the Henry mss out of duty, but I have no hope for it any more. I shall probably pack it in Limbo balls and place it among the lost hopes in the chest of years. Goodbye Henry. I thought you were heroic, but you are only, as was said of you, a babbler of words and rather clumsy about it. . . .

"It is sad when the snow is falling."

Once, during a sudden and massive night snowfall, a mighty roar came from beyond John's cabin. Fear didn't hold him back now. He dashed outside, and, almost before he knew it, was inside the Brigham home from where the violent sounds had seemed to come. He stood there aghast. In the glow of his flashlight, the living room was a mound of jackstraws. Snow was everywhere. It sparkled coldly upon the grand piano, the costly rugs, draperies, everything; and through a great hole in the roof the flakes were still descending. Tons of snow had broken through, buckling the supporting timbers.

John's first thoughts were for the Brigham's great collection of books. He took armload after armload to his cabin, wiped the books carefully, and opened them to dry; house furnishings could wait. As soon as possible, he put a tarpaulin over the damaged roof.

Contrary to a popular version of the incident, which John may have started himself for its story value, he was not fired for "allowing" a tree to crash on the house. The roof had given way simply because of too much snow. Mrs. Brigham held him blameless; shovels would have done little good for snow removal in such a sudden and violent storm. Although John and the family remained friends, the caretaking job came to an abrupt end. He left of his own volition.

During the spring John bought a decrepit 1915 black Dodge roadster. Proud of his forty-dollar bargain, he drove it around to the big fish hatchery near Tahoe City. Lloyd Shebley was impressed and immediately asked if John would drive him to San Francisco on business. On the way, Lloyd talked of his work at the Tahoe City fish hatchery, the newest and best hatchery in the state, and of his impending need for an assistant. John was interested.

While in the Bay City, each splurged and bought a new suit of clothes — Lloyd, a gray flannel; John, a brown Harris tweed. Those suits proved to be more important than they realized.

CHAPTER THIRTEEN

STEINBECK'S arrival for work at the Tahoe City fish hatchery was announced by rattling fenders and a swirl of pine needles and dust. It was Sunday, June 3, 1928. Already familiar with the woodsy grounds, the new hired hand swung his stuttering roadster round the hatchery building to the two-story redwood bachelor's cottage in back. Lloyd Shebley approached on the run.

Reaching into the ancient Dodge only recently bought, John handed out his battered luggage, a typewriter, and some manila envelopes. They lugged the gear inside. Downstairs was a single large room containing a stove, sink, table, and several straight-backed chairs. John said he might do a little writing there, to which Lloyd agreed, but with the reminder that about a million fingerling trout in the hatchery would need nursing care.

Upstairs were two small bedrooms, with toilet and bath between. After stowing John's things, they discussed the next day's routine, when John would officially be on the state payroll at $115 a month. Bert West, the superintendent, lived at the far end of the grounds and wouldn't bother them often. "But you better learn the ropes pronto," Lloyd advised. "Visitors ask the damnedest questions."

Built in 1920, the hatchery, with its high, shingled roof and base of native stone, blended beautifully with the countryside. As John and Lloyd walked there on Monday morning, John asked about an unmarked door at the right of the entrance and learned that it opened into their cubbyhole of an office. He thought it a pity that no sign said so. Inside the hatchery's single vast room were row after row of long troughs. Each held either trout eggs or fingerlings and ran with cold mountain water piped from nearby Walker Springs.

Shebley and Steinbeck got busy. It was feeding time. The recently hatched trout, like newborn calves, received milk, only theirs was clabbered with rennin. For those slightly older, John and Lloyd mixed milk with ground liver, while the diet of the still older fingerlings was ground beef heart. They were fed by the bucketful — and flashed for their morsels like streaks of light. After a spell at the hatchery, they would be released in California lakes or streams.

Among the many duties were the tedious cleanup chores. There was also the job of trapping big lake trout when they ran into a stream to spawn. The hatchery workers had to strip the eggs from the females and milt the males to fertilize the eggs.

One day in the hatchery, as John was feeding ground liver to his impatient brood, he mumbled, "By God, I never thought I'd be midwife to a fish."

Later, Lloyd heard a hammering outside. He investigated and found John tacking a sign on the door of the private office. It read: PISCATORIAL OBSTETRICIAN. John explained it was for the benefit of visitors. Thereafter, when groups of gushing ladies came calling from nearby Tahoe Tavern, they would notice the sign and sometimes address John as "Dr. Steinbeck." At that, he would bow solemnly and start lecturing on the sex life of fish. The only time he broke up was when Lloyd said, "Tell 'em about your forceps job, Doc."

Despite his crowded hours, John had time for other matters — principally girls and writing. Sometimes Shebley would awaken at night to hear John's typewriter clacking in the room below. John had temporarily forsaken pencil and paper in order to hammer out a presentable copy of *Cup of Gold*, which he was anxious to send to New York. But the typing was slow. Shebley could hear an oath now and then and the sound of paper being whipped from the roller.

John found girls less bothersome — sometimes. One evening, after several hours of serious drinking, he took a waitress from Tahoe Tavern to his room. There, an argument developed. Suddenly, downstairs, Lloyd heard the young lady's muffled screams. Dashing upstairs, he burst into John's room and saw his friend leaning from the window, both arms outside and extending downward. John was holding the girl by her ankles, upside-down, her dress, down around her head; he was threatening to let go unless she became "more friendly" — a drop for his guest of a full story. John's face was flushed and contorted.

"Hold on!" Lloyd yelled. "What the hell's the idea?"

John glanced over his shoulder, dead drunk. "Thish cracker-ass keeps sayin' no," he mumbled thickly. "I'll show her!"

"You gone crazy? Just hang on. I'll help."

Between them, they hauled the frightened girl back into the room, where she straightened her clothes and gave John the tongue-lashing of his life. When the tirade was over, Lloyd couldn't resist saying to her, "Good God, you might've landed on your head, miss. Could have killed you. Yeah, and John might have been held for murder."

"What a pity!" the girl said. Then, somewhat calmer, she added in a low voice, "I really wasn't too scared. On the way down, I figured I'd turn over and land on my feet. I'm like a cat that way."

Sobered up, John was contrite, but the experience didn't keep him away from girls — or liquor. To avoid traffic jams in their small bachelors' quarters, John offered a modest proposal: Whenever he or Lloyd had a girl in the house, the upstairs hallway light would be left burning; visible from the driveway, it would serve as a signal to the other to stay away. The warning beacon worked well — so well that Lloyd had to kill many an hour in the shivery outdoors.

Although time-consuming, girls seldom took John's mind completely off the business of authorship. One day John offered to line up a date for a young man named Allan Pollitt, who had come into nearby Truckee on a fish distribution railroad car with a load of trout from Mt. Shasta. What stuck in Pollitt's mind was John's strange behavior that evening with their dates. Whenever the foursome would stop as they drove along the lake, John would admire the view, proceed to heavy petting, then, turning away from the girl completely, would write something in a memo pad. Finally he would rip out the scribbled page and stuff it into an already-filled box.

"What you writing?" the girl asked.

"Oh, notes to myself," John said.

"But why?"

"Just because."

"Because why?"

John looked annoyed. "Some day I'll sort out these memos and write another book. Not very tidy, am I?"

Now it was the girl's turn to be irritated. "You mean, you get ideas for a book when you're — well, when you're making love?"

"That's right," he said.

John's cavalier attitude toward women was soon destined to change. On a day when Shebley had left the hatchery to plant trout in some distant streams, leaving his co-worker alone, two unexpected young women came to visit the hatchery. So completely did they arouse John's interest that he forgot everything else and gave them a personally conducted tour, stretching it beyond all reason and probably inventing a few items to make it last longer. In the process, he became acquainted with Carol Henning and her sister, Idell.

Carol, who especially took his eye, was about twenty-two, five-foot seven or so, with well-defined features, dark brown hair, and expressive blue eyes. She wore her casual clothes with flair, and every move was one of animated grace. Her puckish wit, expressed in language that was a bit salty for a girl, scored instantly with John.

It was nearly six that evening when Lloyd returned from his trout-planting to find John impatiently waiting for him. John told of his visitors, and Lloyd was not surprised to learn that his buddy had arranged a double date for that very evening. Idell, of course, would be for Shebley.

In a race against time, they ate and showered, shaved afresh, and eased into their new suits. Thank God for the new suits, their only presentable attire!

The two sisters, he said, were on vacation at Tahoe for about ten days. Their father was prominent in the building-and-loan business in their hometown of San Jose. Carol's interest was in advertising, art, and design, and at present she was working as a stenographer or secretary for the Schilling tea and coffee company in San Francisco.

As John and Lloyd scrambled into John's battered car, John said that if they drove fast enough they would be on time at McKinney's resort, where the girls were staying. After a few miles, John gave her the gun — and the car thumped along on a flat tire. Groaning, he swerved to the roadside. Like a wild man, he dug out the automobile jack and repair kit while Lloyd hunted up boulders to block the wheels. Out of his handsome new coat, which he promptly dropped on greasy tools, John jacked up the wheel. Off with the tire! Out with the inner tube! Speedily he buffed up the tube, peeled a tire patch from its adhesive backing, applied the patch, pressed — and prayed. It held. By the time they were back in their coats, a good half-hour was gone. But if they hurried, they figured, they wouldn't be *very* late. They started up again, and pretty soon the unbelievable happened. Another flat tire, their second within two miles! They finally reached the girls' cottage at McKinney's resort, disheveled, grimy, and sweaty, their new suits a mess despite all pre-cautions. Their neglected dates greeted them coolly. The boys told their improbable story and retired to clean up, while the girls, looking fresh and lovely in their summer frocks, sighed and waited some more. The evening, which had begun so inauspiciously, ended on the upbeat. There was dancing in the pavilion, and for once John held a girl in his arms who left him dazed.

Never a day went by during the girls' vacation without John and Carol getting together. Sometimes Carol and her sister would dine with the boys in the big downstairs dining room of the hatchery cottage. Occasionally John and Lloyd would take them to nearby Truckee, a fast and loose town of the gold-rush era. Usually starting at the Bucket of Blood, a cellar speakeasy, they would wind up at the reeking, smoke-filled Roma, which John called the "Aroma," where Blind Tom banged the piano for some foxtrotting on the tiny floor. And on some evenings, inasmuch as John had suddenly lost his aversion to dancing, the couples enjoyed that diversion at places on the lake.

Between dates, John's typewriter struck a faster tempo. Carol, Shebley says, was at the keyboard, from which flawless manuscript pages poured forth.

Carol's vacation came to an end shortly after July 4.

A later summer visitor was Polly Smith, daughter of his literary friend in Palo Alto, who had typed and erased her way through the very first draft of *A Lady in Infra-Red*. However, John showed little enthusiasm when they danced at Truckee, and when a cigarette-smoking male brushed against him, burning a tiny hole in his new "courtin' suit," he became furious and produced a borrowed revolver. Polly made him put it away.

The fish-hatchery job ended on August 31, and John took off in his balky Dodge. Parts of that autumn and winter were spent in Salinas and in the little cottage on the Monterey Peninsula. The ever warmer correspondence between John and Carol was fanned by frequent trips to San Francisco to see her. In her spare time she did much of his typing. Then came the electrifying news — at first he couldn't believe it — his novel *Cup of Gold* had been accepted by McBride's! He had sent the manuscript to an old Stanford friend, Amasa (Ted) Miller, then living in the East, who had agreed to act as his agent. The novel had been submitted all over New York — no takers. Then, finally, on the seventh submission, McBride's had given the nod — the same place where he had experienced so much trouble earlier in his writing days.

Buoyed up by this success and now more than ever wanting to have more time with Carol, John moved to San Francisco, where Carol shared an apartment with her sister in an old house on Jackson Street. John's own quarters changed often; he lived in a great variety of rooms.

"I remember a dark little attic on Powell Street. It was in the best tradition with unsheathed rafters and pigeons walking in and out of a small dormer window. Then there was a kind of cave in North Beach completely carpeted wall to wall with garlic. The rest, in my memory were small pads whose only charm lay in cheapness. . . . In such places we learned our trade, or tried to. We had to. Jobs were hard to get. Magazines didn't want our stories. . . . It is true that we learned our trade because there were no better offers but we learned it in the magic heaped on the hills of San Francisco." — *San Francisco Examiner*, November 23, 1958.

While in the Bay City, unable to make a living at writing, Steinbeck took a number of short-lived jobs, including common labor ("at which I was very good"), door-to-door selling ("at which I was lousy"), and department-store clerking. Still, he was happy; Carol was only blocks away.

About this time he began work on an early version of "The Green Lady," the story whose plot he had patterned after his Stanford friend Toby's unsuccessful three-act play. The basis of Toby's plot concerned the hero's love of trees and all growing things — a love that became a psychotic fixation for the forest and eventually led to self-immolation when fire was sweeping his beloved grove. No doubt John's interest was heightened by his own love of trees and his long sojourn among the evergreens of the Tahoe region. The theme, moreover, strengthened his belief that there was a vital relationship between man, the soil, and growing things. At any rate, Toby, frustrated by his second act, amiably withdrew from the project, generously granting John all rights to it — "With no strings attached."

Now calling the story *To an Unknown God* (which would eventually become *To a God Unknown*), Steinbeck made sweeping revisions in characters, structure, episode, and plot. Incidental to its theme in his first go-round was the delightful little story of Rosa and Maria Lopez, vendors extraordinary of tamales and enchiladas. This episode was subsequently removed and later included in *The Pastures of Heaven*, a future book which John was already mulling over even while at work on *Unknown God*. (When *To a God Unknown* was published in 1933, John sent Toby a copy autographed, "For Toby — This isn't much like our old story and yet it is the same story many generations later.")

In the summer of 1929, John and Carol made occasional weekend trips to Palo Alto to visit Dook, who was now studying for his master's degree at Stanford. John always enjoyed these visits with Dook, whose literary judgment he came to appreciate more and more. When Sheffield read something of John's that pleased him, he exulted — aloud. And when he read something of John's that he considered mediocre, he said so.

At John's request, Sheffield did some cursory editing and noted how carefully Steinbeck had toiled with the text of certain manuscript pages to achieve rhythms and tonal effects, revising to eliminate undesirable alliterations and even noticeable sequences of similar vowel sounds in a sentence or series of sentences. All his work showed attention to such details. John was quite amenable to most of the minor changes Dook suggested, but balked at the use of more dashes.

During Carol's vacation in August they camped for two weeks near La Honda in the hills southeast of Half Moon Bay, sleeping on cots in the open though they had an open shelter tent stretched from the side of Carol's patriarchal Buick.

With money not too plentiful, their diet consisted largely of bread, bacon gravy, bacon squares (then selling at ten cents a pound), beans, corn meal, and hamburger (which often could be bought at three pounds for twenty-five cents). When Dook and his wife visited them for a few days, John and Carol were happy they had bought a whole gunnysack of slightly wilted corn on the cob for twenty-five cents. Dook and John discovered crayfish in one of the nearby streams, and, catching a number of them, prepared a magnificent salad, with the help of the girls, using miner's lettuce and onions for the greens.

During the vacation John worked several hours a day on *To an Unknown God*. Immediately after an early breakfast, he set out from camp into the redwood forest carrying an old ledger in which he did his writing, a five-cent bottle of ink, and his penholder with a couple of extra nibs. Since weather was warm, much of the time he wore only sandals and a pair of blue jeans, with the result that he soon acquired a mahogany tan. He preferred to work in a little clearing he had discovered, where the sawed-off stump of a redwood tree served as an excellent writing table. There, surrounded by the huge and ancient trees and the forest silence which even the birds seemed reluctant to break, he wrote rapidly and intently, taking pride in the ridiculously small script which often crowded twenty or more words on a single line. Dook suspected that the minuscule writing was in some way identified with fine craftsmanship and with the idea that delicate and exact expression could not come from a large sprawling hand. Perhaps, too, the tiny letters gave the illusion of secrecy, or at least of the privacy which a writer appreciates. Or maybe, Dook adds, he just liked to write small, particularly as it permitted him thriftily to get many words on a single page.

Some days John produced as many as 3000 words in a session, and largely they were words that remained unchanged in their transition to the printed book. In all his work there are long sequences in which the handwritten original and the published volume are identical.

Part of this sureness and speed came from his habit of carefully thinking through the problems and essentials of the narrative before picking up his pen, and in this he asked and wanted no advice. After he had immersed himself in the characters and mood of the work that lay ahead of him, he would often lie down. Sleep and dreams often served to iron out all the difficulties or even to formulate the exact manner of treatment so that nothing remained but to set it down as fast as his pen would travel.

CHAPTER FOURTEEN

IN August, about the same time as the camping trip, John's first book, *Cup of Gold*. was published. But the breaks were against him. Stuart Rose, the McBride's editor who had been so enthusiastic about the novel, had parted company with the firm after a disagreement, and his successor failed to promote Steinbeck's book. Only a few small advertisements were taken to plug the book, and there were few reviews, all of them terse and perfunctory.

Even the book's dust cover was disappointing. At John's suggestion, it had been designed by his New York friend, Mahlon Blaine. However, Blaine's cover, depicting a flamboyantly dressed pirate, might have been suitable for a boy's book of adventure on the high seas, but it had little appeal for the mature reader. Sales languished. Although John had previously been critical of his own story, he now felt it a conscientious piece of work deserving better treatment and attention. Time, however, brought still another change in his attitude, for seven years later he would write that "outside of a certain lyric quality there isn't much to it."

In the fall of 1929 John went back to the Pacific Grove cottage to concentrate on writing. Other than a $400 advance on *Cup of Gold*, he had only the twenty-five dollars a month provided by his father. Carol subsequently left her San Francisco job and returned to her family home in San Jose, eighty miles from Pacific Grove. Sometimes she and John would see each other, but mostly John stuck to his desk. Pacific Grove was economical. And quiet.

To a God Unknown (now the revised title) was slowly under way. At the same time, *Pastures of Heaven* was taking shape.

In a later year, Dook, then in Long Beach, would receive a package from John — a commercial ledger in which John had written several of his stories. One ledger highlight showed Steinbeck starting a practice he would follow through life, his indulgence in "warmup exercises" by writing footnotes to a friend — in this case to Dook. The footnotes also served as an excellent, if unintentional, Steinbeck showcase, revealing the depths of his emotions and his dedication to a friend.

The 12 x 7½-inch commercial ledger was bound in gray cloth and originally purchased for eighty-two cents at Holman's Department Store. In the front and back was printed such tantalizing information as weight per bushel of grain, carrying capacity of a freight car, quantity of seed required to plant an acre, and postal regulations. The body of the ledger, consisting of 300 numbered pages of thirty-eight lines per page, had been used by John for the penning of several short items and two stories — *Pastures of Heaven* and *To a God Unknown*.

The stories are written in the familiar minute script, averaging from ten to more than twenty words per line. In various portions of the book, different-colored inks appear, from purple to green to blue-black. Written on the flyleaf is a rough index of the contents and a listing of the eleven narratives of *Pastures of Heaven*. Only two other items are mentioned: "Unnamed Narrative" and "New Novel." There is also the notation: "With footnotes to Dook."

The "Unnamed Narrative" runs a scant three pages while the "New Novel," which is *To a God Unknown*, fills most of the remaining pages.

Immediately following *Pastures* is the first note to Sheffield.

To Dook

When I bought this book, and began to fill it with words it occurred to me that you might like to have it when it was full. You have that instinct so highly developed in magpies, pack rats and collectors. If this were a blank book, you would probably like it better. I can imagine you keeping a book blank because of your hatred of change. In spite of all this, I should like you to have this book and my reasons are all sentimental and therefore, of course, unmentionable. I love you very much. I have never been able to give you a present that cost any money. It occurs to me that you might accept a present that cost me a hell of a lot of work. For I do not write easily. Three hours of writing requires twenty hours of preparation. Luckily I have learned to dream about the work, which saves me some working time.

What I wanted to say was this. Up to this page the stories are the best I can do at the present time. Now the series is through and I'm going to take two months vacation. In that time I shall try six or seven short stories, light, amusing and restful. I may even try to sell some of them and if I do, it will be under a mom [sic] de plume. So I'm asking you to keep quiet and mouselike about the stories which follow this. I'll make a note when the ban is off.

[Then this note:]

Now a month is gone and the stories have never materialized. The next is a fragment and then begins a narrative built from the ruins of the *Unknown God*. I hope it will be better.

[The "fragment" begins the story of a little boy named Mizpah living in Pacific Grove. After about 1600 words, the tale trails off, and a large "OUT", triply underlined, appears below it. Then another note, almost an invocation, intensely emotional:]

Again

Now the new work starts — a good plan, a good story; strong, sturdy standing with fine legs set wide, and contemplating the wreckage of the earth-body. His chin is down and his bewildered eyes look at the ground. And then his active love arises a force as mighty as the thrust in the thighs of a bull when he drives the invincible phallus into the quivering yoni. And the love grows like a black rain until he rains the good blood from his throat upon the dying earth.

Now as always — humility and terror. Fear that the working of my pen cannot capture the grinding of my brain. It is so easy to understand why the ancients prayed for the help of a muse. And the Muse came and stood beside them. And we, heaven help us, do not believe in Muses. We have nothing to fall back on but our own craftsmanship and it, as modern literature attests, is inadequate.

We might be wrong. Somewhere in a cave dug by the young and insolent brains of our times a spirit who delights in literature might languish. Some immortal intelligence there may be which understands the hunger man has for beauty. If such there is, may my words be burned with the flame of my desire to produce some beautiful thing before I die and am sucked into the hungry earth.

My story is better than I am. It seems to be contrived by a better brain than I possess. If I hoped enough and prayed enough, might not the spirit which helped me to design my plan, help me to bring it into the land.

May I be honest; may I be decent; may I be unaffected by the technique of hucksters. If invocation is required, let this be my invocation — may I be strong and yet gentle, tender and yet wise, wise and yet tolerant. May I for a little while, only for a little while, see with the inflamed eyes of a god.

[That footnote was evidently intended to introduce Dook to the new version of *To an Unknown God*, but the following fifteen pages are cut from the book, indicating that the first start at the new novel was destroyed. A new beginning was made, and this apparently satisfied the writer, for the story carries through until finished. Along the way, in the inch of space at the top of various pages, appear progress footnotes.]

Well — how do you like it so far. It seems strange how the thing grows, how the people become more essentially real than the people I know. This is a week's work from the beginning. I am going very fast — too fast I'm afraid. But my story is impatient. Besides, I have said that I will submit it by July and this is the end of the (next page)

[But there is no continuation on the next page. Instead, further along, is the following:]

These heads make good places for notes. I wonder how you'll like this book, whether Joseph will be to you the person he is to me. Of course that is impossible. It seems very strange that this book will be finished before I see you again. I think this is a better, tighter story than any I've done yet.

[Halfway through Chapter 8 appears one of the longest and most charming of the footnotes:]

An examination of this mss., should anyone be interested, should be of interest to the camp-followers of literature, the change of ink colors, for example, might to those students of influences in the life of an artist, be of the rarest significance. This volume begins in purple ink — my mood was rich with the blood of youth, rich with the intricacy of style. I was beginning to feel the purple of the Caesar. Then suddenly the ink changes to green. Old Nature, bless her. The trees and all the green earth, stems straining to lay their leaves in heaven. Youth again but green youth, not the earth purple, the soil purple, the purple of seeds — but the green of growth toward what comes now — the blue — of heaven — of the mysterious end — the finish — blue of philosophy, of quiet maturity. Indeed, there is room for thought in all this. And lest some god dam fool should devote time to this subject which might better be employed say in a concordance on Zane Grey, I shall explain. A year ago Holman's department store had an ink sale — ink that had been so long in stock that it was as ripe and rich as Napoleon brandy, cobwebs on the bottles. Two bottles for five cents. I bought two and used them. On page 167 the green was exhausted and I went back, but the sale was over and I bought one bottle of blue for ten cents. Purple of the soil, green of growth, blue ten cents. Media are ridiculous. And Duke — should you ever look over this book which I am intending you should have, if I have as good a story as I think I have, you may have a little chuckle to yourself. For you know that only the end counts

This story has grown since I started it. From a novel about people, it has become a novel about the world. And you must never tell it. Let it be found out. The new eye is being opened here in the west — the new seeing. It is probable that no one will know it for two hundred years. It will be confused, analyzed, analogized, criticized, and none of our fine critics will know what is happening. I could name four who know, one with his brain and three with their bodies. This must be cryptic.

Duke, this novel is just under way. I don't know how it will be when it is finished. That's funny, isn't it? If you ever see this the birthing pains will be over. And here I am sitting and wondering how I can bring off the thing. All the scenes aren't born yet. It would be much less fun if it were sure. There are things in my mind as strong as pure as good as anything in the structure of literature. If I do not put them down, it will be because I have not the technique. The story is too big, Duke. I am so afraid of it sometimes — so fearful of its implications that I am tempted to burn it as an over-evil thing. And it is not evil. It is good and timeless. Joseph is a giant shouldering his way among the ages, pushing the stars aside to make a passage to god. And this god — that is the thing. When god is reached — will anybody believe it. It really doesn't matter. I believe it and Joseph believes it. The story is a parable, Duke. The story of a race, growth and death. Each figure is a population, and the stones, the trees, the muscled mountains are the world — but not the world apart from man — the world *and* man — the one inseparable unit man plus his environment. Why they should ever have been misunderstood as being separate I do not know. Man is said to come out of his environment. He doesn't know when. Now this note is over.

[On a later page:]

Note: I wonder how you are liking it now. There seems to be no end to my excitement on this theme. The pass is my pit next to the circle in the pines. But the circle in the pines, as you have no doubt surmised, is the citadel of the story. Curious! I am adding these notes as though you might be reading this from mss. and it is probable that you will never look through this book. But it does me good to talk thus to you now and then and it does the mss. no harm. There are beautiful things to come. I wonder if you know why I address this manuscript to you. You are the only person in the world who believes I can do what I set out to do. Not even I believe that all the time. And so, in a kind of gratitude I address all my writing to you, whether or not you know it.

[The final entry comes at the conclusion of *To an Unknown God.*]

Note: Now this book is finished Dook. You will have to work on it; to help straighten out the roughness, to say where it falls short. It will be much better when your work on it is done. In giving you this manuscript I do not give you anything I value very highly. I wish I valued it more so that it would be a better gift. The book had plans beyond my abilities I'm afraid. It isn't nearly all I hoped it would be. But it is finished anyway and done with. You haven't read it yet. I hope you will like it some. I remember when I finished the earlier book of the same title. I took it to you and you said, "It is very good." And I knew you knew it was terrible and you knew I knew you knew it. And if this one is as bad I hope you will tell me. I know it isn't as a matter of fact. I know enough of technique to be sure it is much better constructed. But I've worked too hard on it. I can't tell much about it.

Anyway — this is your book now. I hope you'll like to have it.

love John

CHAPTER **FIFTEEN**

J OHN'S literary horizons widened in 1930, thanks to the interest of his old friend and mentor in Palo Alto, E.C.A. Smith. Ever since his Stanford days, where she had offered advice and encouragement, she had recognized his writing potential and maintained an active interest in his work. Now she advised him to send *Pastures of Heaven*, when he was ready, to her own literary agents, McIntosh and Otis, a relatively new firm which had already sold several of her manuscripts. The agency was headed by Mavis McIntosh, who would leave the firm in the 1940s, and Elizabeth Otis. John communicated with them at once, the beginning of a happy alliance that would continue throughout his writing career. His first submission, however, came later.

Literary efforts were temporarily sidetracked during the year when he and Carol became interested in a new plastic moulage process introduced to them by Ritchie Lovejoy. The young man had discovered a Swiss product named Negocol, which opened up a new and easier way of making casts of faces, hands, and other objects. It was a collodial, rubbery substance supplied in large "crumbs" at a cost of eight dollars for a two-pound package. Fairly low heat would change the material to a thick paste, which, when cooled to about ninety degrees, set rapidly and dried to a glossy, elastic surface. Unlike plaster of Paris, it did not cling to things it touched, making unnecessary the customary heavy greasing required for plaster casts of the human face. Lovejoy became sold on its artistic possibilities. Enthusiastic over the results, Lovejoy and his wife Tal, demonstrated some of the uses of Negocol to John and Carol, who were also intrigued. The foursome began formulating a project which promised fame and fortune.

For some reason, they decided to launch their venture in Los Angeles. John wrote excitedly to Dook, who, then living in Eagle Rock while teaching at Occidental College, invited John and Carol to stay at his home while setting up their new enterprise.

And that was the start of the Faster Master Plaster Casters.

Dook's innocent invitation, approved by his wife Maryon, resulted in half the state's population moving into the Sheffield home. The first to arrive was Nadja (Nadjezda), the pretty and highly emotional sister of Tal. That night the Lovejoys arrived; next, briefly, came Mahlon Blaine, then Archie (Arjuna) Strayer of Pasadena, a former student of Dook's. Word of the "open house" had spread like wildfire. Finally John and Carol arrived. Carol's Buick had succumbed on the way, and somehow, probably by trading it in and borrowing from their scant supply of cash, they had acquired a battered Marmon. The girls and Lovejoy became the chief technicians of the new art project; Blaine, its art director; and Strayer, business manager. Dook, the only one with a real job, was the provider of funds, although funds were always low.

The hillside house consisted of a spacious living room, one small bedroom, a screened sleeping porch, a large kitchen, a tiny utility room, and a wide, covered front veranda which could sleep a number of guests, as could the living room. Even so, seven persons and three cats tended to strain residential capacities.

The newcomers' thirst seemed unslakable. Dook brewed his own beer, but the supply was rapidly exhausted. He stepped up production to ten gallons every five days and still could barely keep up with consumption. The skin began peeling from his fingers. John suggested he quit his teaching job and become a full-time brewmaster.

The excitable, uninhibited sisters drank everything in sight and loved singing, dancing, loud music, and boisterous games. Dook's wife frequently wrestled with Carol. The cats slept on everybody except John, who detested them and hurled them away with imprecations. Between times, occasionally, came cat screeches from beneath the many moving and unpredictable feet. All this had an adverse effect upon John's halfhearted attempts to write and upon Dook's efforts to grade college papers. Both nearly gave up — and sometimes did to join the fun.

Meanwhile, the Faster Master Plaster Casters got off to a staggering start. In the initial experiments the group suffered many minor crises. They found that when a mold had been taken of a face, the weight of the small amount of plaster poured into it would spread the elastic Negocol, resulting in a distorted cast. The problem was solved by applying bracings and crosshatchings of cloth. They learned to make an entire head in two molds. To their dismay they discovered that a plaster head looked larger than the original, though it was of exactly the same size; that a cast of a thin face looked thinner, or a full face fatter than the original, so they had to make careful adjustments before pouring the plaster.

Their agenda was vague but optimistic. Steinbeck thought there should be a good market for personalized masks of individuals, made and furnished to order like photographs or portraits. Young movie stars might buy, they all felt.

But Negocol was expensive, and so was plaster of Paris in the quantities used. Needing demonstration pieces, they made a fine mask of Tal, and, by adding twisted horns, produced a delightful faun. Steinbeck, always sensitive about reproductions of himself, was reluctant to serve as a model but finally agreed. The results were horrifying, and he destroyed the mask.

Away at school most of the day, busy making beer at other times, Dook could be of little help, but Lovejoy got busy and succeeded in luring the first (and only one) of their movie starlets to the studio for a portrait mask. She was a round-cheeked lass who came accompanied by the brother of Ricardo Cortez, a leading male actor of the time; he was skeptical about the whole project. But the taking of the mask went without a hitch. Results weren't so encouraging. In the cast the girl's well-filled cheeks looked like apples, and no tricks of paint could reduce them. She and her escort stalked out without paying.

The finest mask was of a student of Dook's, who had ideal facial contours. Blaine did an unusually good job of delicate coloring, and the result was lovely, the mask surpassing the beauty of the girl herself.

That triumph should have marked the beginning of success for the Faster Master Plaster Casters, but, apart from a few later experiments, it was the last real achievement. Strayer, the business manager, suddenly revealed that his expense account was gone and credit strained to the limit. He quit. Blaine and Lovejoy became temperamental. Steinbeck was tired of the whole thing; anyway, he wanted to write more. Ritchie, Tal, and Nadja moved into a nearby house. Sheffield was by this time getting disgusted, and, with the multiple departures, the whole project collapsed. With everybody gone, John, Carol, and the Sheffields sighed with relief as the house settled down to normal. John liked to see some semblance of order, and frequently, after regarding the condition of the floor, would get the broom and sweep violently. The fact that he usually raised a cloud of dust and always left the sweepings in a pile in the center of the room did not detract from his good intentions. He and Carol often took over the cooking.

After two or three months, John and Carol decided to get married, although Dook believes that had been their original intention on coming south. What really inspired the decision was that they had found a house, for, Carol decreed, it wasn't proper to have a house of one's own without being married. The house didn't look like much. Although it had walls, floors, and a roof of sorts, there were great gaps in all of them — windows were broken, plumbing run down, dirt ankle-deep. After studying the shack, John believed he could make it habitable and offered fifteen dollars a month rent, as is. The owner agreed. Luckily, it was only a short distance from the Sheffield place, so that John could work on it whenever he wanted, and occasionally the Sheffields helped.

After John had removed the broken furniture and miscellaneous junk, he and Carol went after the rest with shovels. Then, at Carol's inspiration, they cut out much of the front of the house and installed a huge multipaned window acquired from a wrecking company. Although at first baffled by the mysteries of plumbing, John eventually had gas and water pipes working. As a particular triumph, he bought a secondhand water heater for ten dollars which he repaired and made usable.

While John installed or replaced various pieces of builders' hardware, patched the roof, and coped with things like chimneys and doors, Carol was busy with floors and walls. Determined scrubbing with lye revealed a floor of sound planking. It was sanded, waxed, and rubbed until it gleamed.

At a secondhand store they bought a small leather-covered divan and next acquired a secondhand box springs and mattress, which, placed under the picture window and draped with a colorful Mexican blanket, served as an ample divan by day and a bed by night. John patched up some old furniture, while Carol assembled bright curtains, rugs, and hangings. But, as they were adding the finishing touches, the thought of the impending marriage ceremony made them increasingly uneasy — something about licenses and rituals frightened them both. The house was almost ready for occupancy, but Carol still vowed that she wouldn't move into it without being married.

Eventually the Sheffields talked them into getting a license — and discovered they had two neurotics on their hands. When John and Carol refused to make any preparations or even so much as discuss it, other than to vow that they wouldn't enter any goddamned church, Maryon Sheffield took the initiative and made tentative arrangements with the justice of the peace in downtown Glendale. As all four headed for his office, both Carol and John had a heavy case of the jitters and kept urging their companions to take them home so they could compose themselves.

On January 14, 1930, deaf to entreaties, the Sheffields parked in front of a big building on Colorado Street near Brand, made them get out of the car, and half-wrestled them through the doorway and into the elevator. Fortunately, there was no delay in the office of Judge Harry W. Chase — he was expecting the foursome and ready to go to work immediately. So the foursome stood before him while he read the brief civil ceremony — John completely rigid, with one eyebrow raised nearly to the hairline and a voice that almost broke as he made the responses, and Carol twisting her face to suppress hysterical giggles. With extreme dignity, Steinbeck paid the judge his fee, accepted congratulations, and then broke for the open air as if on the verge of suffocation.

Feeling expansive by then, Dook offered to stand everyone to a wedding meal — "sky's the limit!" At a nearby cut-rate eatery Dook splurged on hamburgers for everyone — not the ordinary ten-cent variety, either, but the deluxe fifteen-centers with a slab of cheese in the middle. The postnuptial good humor was of short duration. By the time they got back to the Sheffield house, the newlyweds were snapping profanely at each other and would probably have worked up to a violent fight if Dook and Maryon hadn't intervened. The Sheffields ushered the Steinbecks to their new house, but John didn't carry his bride over the threshold.

CHAPTER SIXTEEN

a MEASURE of domestic tranquillity having returned, John was ready to resume writing. Putting aside other literary efforts, he began in earnest to work on a long-considered novel. Dook describes its genesis and theme: In wrestling with the characters in his various writings, John had become fascinated with the problems of personality, especially with the idea that personalities are not fixed and stable, but subject to and influenced by the interpretations of the observer, almost as if the two were chemicals interacting on each other, often changing the original form of each. Many other factors enter the picture, such as prejudices, circumstances, social and economic relationships, and so on.

John knew, of course, that the idea was far from new; in one form or another, it had influenced much literature and the most elementary psychology. But he found endless ramifications, as well as what might be a key to understanding, manipulation, and depiction of character.

The central figure of the book, John decided, was to be a man with the general characteristics of his father — a kind man, honest, reserved, strong-minded, imaginative, and gently humorous. But instead of being a protagonist in the literal sense, he was never to appear in his own person, save perhaps through excerpts from a diary. The book, as planned, would start with a simple statement of his death, perhaps through an obituary in a small-town newspaper. From there on, his good friends were to tell of the man as they had known him, with their interpretations not only of his deeds, character, and motives but also of the other individuals who made up his circle of associates. Among such apologists were to be his wife, his son and/or daughter, his business partner, his secretly maintained mistress, his best friend, his servant, with perhaps one of his parents, a lodge brother, a business rival, and others. Thus, each individual would present pictures of the central figure, of himself, and of all other characters, and all estimates would differ from the others. The intertwining structural pattern delighted John, as did the intrinsic irony, the kaleidoscopic shift in point of view, and the composite character which he hoped to produce while attacking the concept of an absolute and immutable truth.

The tentative title of his 30,000-word manuscript was *Dissonant Symphony*. At a later date, he would mail it to McIntosh and Otis. But the limitations imposed by such a form rankled him and he eventually became unhappy with his characterization. In Dook's opinion, John's deep-seated love and admiration for his father, who was still alive, may have produced feelings of guilt.

In 1933 he withdrew the story, telling his agents that he was ashamed of it and wouldn't want it published. In the opinion of critic Lewis Gannett, John Steinbeck, at this time, was "groping, experimenting, finding his way."

Automobile trouble provided a different sort of experimentation in John's Eagle Rock days. When something went wrong with the ten-year-old Marmon Special, John went to work on it and, after disassembling the rear axle, discovered that a new ring gear was needed. Eventually he found a secondhand replacement in a wrecking yard and after long hours of labor managed to get it snugly in place.

Several nights later, John and Carol started out to visit friends across town, but the car shuddered to a stop. When the vehicle was towed to a garage, the gear was found improperly installed and ruined forever. Disgustedly, John made a deal with the garage owner and came away with a rickety, topless Chevrolet touring car, built about 1923. Although its radiator leaked badly and needed constant refilling, the auto ran fairly well. It also provided the inspiration for a usable story idea.

Having been told that a little cornmeal in the radiator was a remedy for leaks, he dumped in plenty before a twenty-two-mile trip to Santa Monica with Carol and the Sheffields. Before long, the radiator was steaming hot as they moved along thoroughfares black with traffic. On Wilshire Boulevard, the worst happened. The radiator cap flew off with a bang, followed by a tremendous geyser of yellow mush. The goop splattered onto the windshield, onto Carol, onto their guests, even onto passing cars.

The mush geyser served fine for his story, *A Model-T Named "It."* In this piece he substituted *oatmeal* as his radiator corrective, and when the sloppy explosion came in his old car, according to the article, he was riding with his mother, who was dressed in her best. ("We drove through downtown Los Angeles erupting mush, my mother scraping it out of her eyes. I never saw so much mush. I never saw my mother so mad." — *Ford Times*, July 1953.)

Behind the Sheffield house a long slope, with no neighbors close on either side of the backyard, provided an ideal spot for sun bathing. Screened off with canvas and gunnysacks, and with several mattresses to sit on, the shielded solar pavilion drew many of Dook's and Maryon's friends. Sometimes, six or eight of them would be there at the same time, basking in the nude, sweating, and passing a cold pitcher of beer.

On one occasion, with only the Sheffields and the Steinbecks present, and while John slept soundly on a mattress, Maryon and Carol decided on a bold prank. Suppressing their giggles, they approached John with several narrow, colorful ribbons and ever so cautiously tied them into bows on his pubic hairs. As they did so, he stirred restlessly one or twice but didn't awaken. When at last he did open his eyes, he yawned, stretched, got to his feet, and broke into a little barefoot jig. Meanwhile, his spectators were laughing openly, contagiously.

"What's so funny?" John demanded.

"You know," said Dook, "you're almost handsome today, all dolled up that way."

It was then John discovered the adornments. Instead of being annoyed, he gazed upon the handiwork admiringly, expressed appreciation, and wore his pretty pigtails all afternoon.

Another touch of vanity, real or pretended, came one afternoon when all four were again sunning themselves, the wives planning to try out the bleaching properties of strong peroxide and ammonia. One of them suggested testing the solution on John's hair, which was normally dark, coarse, and wavy. He was willing. So the girls applied successive, well-drenched packs to his head, and each pack turned his hair pinker and pinker until it was a brilliant, flaming sunset, shot through with salmon tints and wavering gold.

As with the pigtails, John showed no trace of indignity. Unlike the pigtails, however, there was no shedding this gift, nor did he want to. Over Carol's protests that he must do something, he insisted that he wanted to wear his hair that way.

Several days later the quartet took off for the seashore to visit John's sister Mary, now married with children and living in southern California. John drove, his wild multihued mop flashing like a beacon in the topless Chevy. Drivers stared open-mouthed, snarling traffic, following him with their eyes as long as possible. At the meeting place on the beach, John's outraged sister deliberately ignored him, while her two children, shrieking, tugged at his locks to see if they were real.

A week later John yielded to Carol's pleading and dyed his hair jet black, which was every bit as startling as before.

The honeymoon cottage, small as it was, made them both very happy, and their constant improvements became the envy of the neighborhood. Their only income was from John's father and occasional small sums from relatives, but with astute management on Carol's part they made out comfortably. The biggest bite was the fifteen dollars a month for rent. The writing was going well.

But their little paradise was not to last. They had lived there only a short time when the owner of the property came to town. He visited the house and hardly believed what he saw. What had once been the town eyesore had become an immaculate cottage fronted by a lawn and well-kept flower bed. Even the plumbing worked.

The Steinbecks, he decreed, would have to go. Suddenly it seemed he would need the place for his son and his bride. But Mr. and Mrs. Steinbeck could take as long as a full month to pack and get out, he generously said. No hurry.

Their next two residences came in quick succession — the first, a dark little house a few blocks from Dook's home, on the western edge of Glendale; the second, a somewhat less stifling place on the Coast Range foothills in La Cañada district, near an earthquake fault. At least, the latter dwelling wasn't lonely, having occasional, and not altogether unwelcome, visitations from a real honest-to-goodness poltergeist — or so John swore. He and Carol reported all sorts of spooky phenomena — locked doors creaking open in the middle of the night, footsteps in unoccupied parts of the house, pictures swinging on the walls, mysterious thumpings. Not easily frightened, they soon became rather proud of their private ghost.

However, this constant moving, the intrusion of poltergeists, and the everlasting shortage of funds were anything but conducive to writing. John continued to work hard on short stories, but destroyed nearly all of them. It was a disheartening period for him, underscored by his failure to make any commercial headway.

It was no surprise to the Sheffields when John and Carol became fed up. With winter approaching, they loaded their old car, shipped other belongings, and departed.

CHAPTER SEVENTEEN

SURE I remember the Nineteen Thir-
ties, the terrible troubled, triumphant, surging Thirties. I can't think of
any decade in history when so much happened in so many directions."
— "A Primer on the 30's," first published in *Esquire Magazine*, June
1960.

John had chosen one of the toughest of all times to bear down on
writing — in the Great Depression period of the early Thirties. He was
well aware that when people are in dire straits generally the first things
they do without are new books. All across the country book stores were
folding; publishers were hard-hit and jittery. Even so, John thought he
had a sweating chance to make it. Despite the bleak economic picture,
several things were going in his favor. The three-room cottage in Pacific
Grove which he and Carol occupied from late 1930 to the early part of
1932 may have been tiny, but it was provided by his father rent-free and
he still received a small monthly allowance from home.

His constant state of semi-poverty, combined with an admitted
squeamishness, led John to put off dental attention as long as he possibly
could. He and Carol had been settled in the Pacific Grove cracker-box
home only a short while when his throbbing jaw finally drove him to a
dentist's office in New Monterey. His dragging feet landed him in the
office just in time to meet an individual who would play a vital role in his
life.

John was bracing himself in the dentist's waiting room when the
door to the treatment cubicle opened and a patient emerged, swearing.
He was wiry, his movements quick, and in his hand was a recently
extracted molar attached to an unpleasant fragment of jawbone.

". . . [the patient] held the reeking relic out to me and said, 'Look at
that god-damned thing.' I was already looking at it. 'That came out of
me.' . . .

"That was the first time I ever saw him. I had heard that there was an interesting man in town who ran a commercial laboratory, had a library of good music, and interests wider than invertebratology. I had wanted to come across him for some time." — "About Ed Ricketts," *The Log from the Sea of Cortez.*

Edward F. Ricketts, "a slight man with a beard," was a marine biologist and a good one, who owned and operated a remodeled old structure on Cannery Row called the Pacific Biological Laboratories, a haphazardly run biological supply house. He had mussed-up brown hair and brown eyes. His worn and tweedy coat looked too tight. John liked him instantly. Their friendship developed rapidly and remained unwavering through the years. Eventually John would dedicate four books to him and put him in six novels, depicting him as Friend in *Burning Bright,* as Doc in *Cannery Row,* Doc Burton in *In Dubious Battle,* Jim Casey in *Grapes of Wrath,* Doc Winter in *The Moon is Down,* and Doc in *Sweet Thursday.*

Daily at the Steinbeck cottage, after his teeth were fixed, John bent over his cheap ledgers, formalizing in his delicate script the plots and characters that had been germinating in his mind for a long time. Sometimes he tried dictating to Carol. All in all, it was a strange fiction factory and the wildest sort of gamble.

Early in 1931 Steinbeck announced to his agents his theme for *Pastures of Heaven,* as a story he had already written once or twice and was now reworking. Its setting would be the Corral de Tierra, a valley in the hills about twelve miles from Monterey (the region of his sandstone castles), which he was calling Las Pastures del Cielo to avoid any possible identification with its real inhabitants. The book, he said, would consist of a series of stories, each complete in itself, but all held together thematically. The story was sent to McIntosh and Otis later that year, his first submission to the agency, and was enthusiastically received. From the very beginning, the agency had great faith in its new client. Out of this mutual respect a sincere friendship developed. Indeed, over the years the letters between them took on the warm, personal nature of family correspondence; Steinbeck would stay with them throughout his life.

During this same period, he sent in "Dissonant Symphony," the story he later withdrew. In need of quick money, he ground out a potboiler titled *Murder at Full Moon,* a mystery thriller aimed strictly at the pulps. He signed it with the pseudonym "John Stonebrook." Laid in the swamps and fields of Castroville, the story concerned a man who turned lunatic at full moon and was pursued by a potbellied sleuth resembling a potato bug. Steinbeck later withdrew this piece, saying it was no good and that he wanted to forget the damned thing.

In January of '32 he tentatively started a thorough revision of *God Unknown*, but interruptions delayed its completion for a year. He would not submit the final work until a year later.

Meanwhile, in Pacific Grove, he was becoming acquainted with some of the local inhabitants who would refuel his imagination for future stories. There were long talks with Susan M. Gregory, who taught English, Latin, and Spanish at the Monterey high school, and visits with old Mrs. Harriet Gragg, whose father had settled in California in 1837. From both Sue Gregory and Mrs. Gragg he was absorbing much color about the *paisanos,* happy-go-lucky people of mixed Spanish, Mexican, Indian, and Caucasian blood who lived principally upon the slopes behind Monterey — "where the forest and town intermingle." Originally he had planned to write some short stories about these "people of laughter and kindness," such as he had done back at Stanford with the little piece on Sweets Ramirez and her sweeping machine. Now, instead, he envisioned putting them in a novel whose incidents would be tied together with a knights-of-the-round-table theme. The idea appealed to him strongly, for he would be making some practical use of his long and continuing study of Arthurian times. Best of all, the book would in no way conflict with his long-range plan to do a major work, some day, on the age of chivalry. Nothing must interfere with that. Now, though, Sue Gregory was his best bet for immediate information.

Descendant of old Spanish-English families, Sue Gregory had a love of teaching and of books that came naturally. Her grandfather, W.E.P. Hartnell, founded Hartnell College near Salinas, the first institution of higher learning in the state. One of her two brothers was Jackson Gregory, the author of Westerns, and the other was a teacher. The clincher for John was that she herself was a poet of talent.

A story about one of her brothers grabbed John's ear. Offered a job in a typical one-room schoolhouse in the gold-rush country, he was warned in advance about the rowdy youngsters there. Many instructors had come and gone. He took the job anyway. On the first day of school, when he called his class to order, the roughhouse started. Without a word, the new teacher opened his desk drawer, pulled out a .45-caliber revolver, aimed at an open window across the room, and fired. The blast shook the room. Calmly he laid his cannon on the desk and again called for order. There was no more trouble.

But Sue's stories about the *paisanos* were the most fascinating of all

Typical of the now demolished houses on Tortilla Flat

(right)
The former Carol Henning,
John's first wife, who
patiently typed and retyped
The Grapes of Wrath
and other of John's early
stories. She was a talented
as an artist and poet
in her own right.

E.C.A. Smith, who wrote
under the masculine
pen name of "John Breck,"
was a milepost in Steinbeck's
literary life. Because of her
he joined McIntosh and Otis,
N.Y. literary agents.

Ed Ricketts on one of
his "dress up days." The
photo, his son's favorite,
was taken in 1942.

(right)
John Steinbeck —
photo used in
promotion of
The Moon is Down

(below)
Cronies since boyhood —
John Steinbeck (left)
and Max Wagner in
bombed-out London

Arched eyebrow
was a familiar
expression of
John Steinbeck's

John with wife
No. 2, Gwyn Conger,
in the town square
at Cuernavaca,
Mexico, during the
filming of
The Pearl

Adoring John Steinbeck with Elaine, the former Mrs. Zachary Scott, wife No. 3, on a visit to the courtyard of the Doge's Palace in Venice.

The sandstone castles
of Corral de Tierra

John Steinbeck and
President Lyndon B. Johnson

Elaine and John Steinbeck arriving in Moscow in 1963
on a cultural exchange trip for President Kennedy

John Steinbeck looks as though he might eat up Carl Sandburg,
but these two Nobel prize winners were good friends

The cozy octagonal writing room built by John
on his estate in Sag Harbor, Long Island.
Much writing in his later years was done here.

John inside the octagonal writing room

to John, who couldn't get enough of them. It was to Susan Gregory he dedicated *Tortilla Flat*.

Another side of the story came from Mrs. Gragg, who would dwell upon the pride and dignity of the Mexicans and Spanish whom she had known so intimately ever since childhood. John took abundant notes.

In the summer of 1932, with the customary restlessness upon him, John and Carol again headed for southern California, and again had big ideas which they believed couldn't miss. There was good news to take along on the trip. Robert O. Ballou had accepted *Pastures of Heaven*. It didn't matter that the New York book world was in turmoil and that publishing houses were changing hands overnight; Ballou was wildly enthusiastic — so enthusiastic that he would write publisher Martin Secker in London that the story was "one of the most distinguished novels I ever read in manuscript." The publication date was set for that autumn.

In southern California, Steinbeck's "big ideas" all went sour, one after another, until abject poverty threatened. He had hoped to write and sell stories of local interest but it didn't work out. In search of color, he wrote the government of Mexico for permission to ride horseback through 400 miles of that country, but never made the trip. Other plans fizzled, too.

Meanwhile, McIntosh and Otis were urging him to finish *To a God Unknown*. However, that effort had to be postponed. Dire poverty necessitated taking a job. (When the final version of the story was mailed in February 1933, he predicted it would be hard to sell.) The electric company was threatening to shut off his power for lack of payment, and in a few days his rent would be up. He and Carol were living in a little shack roofed with tar paper in the less desirable part of Laguna Beach, below the Three Arches.

As though money problems weren't worry enough, John received upsetting news from home. His mother, intermittently troubled with high blood pressure, had taken a turn for the worse. It was March, of course! March! The month she had always superstitiously dreaded. ("She practically held her breath until it was over every year." — *Journal of a Novel.*)

During their days in the tar-paper shack John was visited by a reporter from the weekly *Laguna Beach Life*, a young woman who had heard of *Pastures of Heaven* (then in the book stores but selling poorly). She wanted to know Mr. Steinbeck's philosophy. Remembering his own newspaper days, and the stumbling blocks when people wouldn't talk, he decided to give the interviewer something to write about, even if he had to invent it.

Seated under a tree in the yard with Carol and the girl, sipping coffee, John orated with tongue-in-cheek on the need for redemption of the human spirit, even wildly pleading for a return of blood sacrifices. The girl was wide-eyed. Finally she snapped shut her notebook and triumphantly hurried away to tell the world, or at least Laguna Beach, about Steinbeck the madman.

CHAPTER **EIGHTEEN**

BACK in Pacific Grove in the spring of 1933, John and Carol picked up right where they had left off. Although they were again living in the tiny rent-free house, times were even tougher than before. But they had plenty of company. Twelve million people were jobless across the land. Bread lines stretched everywhere.

John's short stories went out regularly and just as regularly came back, but usually with encouraging words from McIntosh and Otis. Despite the rejections, his agents knew he was hitting a stride that couldn't long be overlooked.

Of principal interest in those days was his developing story about the *paisanos*. Sometimes John and Carol and a few others, all equally broke, would attend paisano parties in Seaside, where they met old friends, made new ones, and danced to the music of accordion and violin. It made for a cheap evening.

As formerly, he often visited Mrs. Gragg. But his primary source of *paisano* lore and color remained Susan Gregory. By now, she was keeping a dossier on what she saw and heard, and since her schoolwork kept her in close contact with the *paisano* kids, her note-taking was never scant. With friends in Monterey one memorable evening, she heard a police siren screaming uphill behind the town, toward sloping Johnson Street. Everyone fell silent, listening. Attorney and ex-mayor Carmel Martin was the first to speak. "There must be hell poppin' on Tortilla Flat," he said.

The name clicked. Sue made a note and later repeated it to John. He was elated. Tortilla Flat! Tortilla Flat! He had heard that name before, but now it dawned that here was his title.

Sue and Mrs. Gragg, however, were not his only sources of information, for he mingled with the *paisanos* on the waterfront, drank with them, and delighted in their antics.

On many evenings friends dropped over from Carmel. On these occasions, Steinbeck was usually the center of some fiery dispute. He delighted in stoking debates with unorthodox views. And sometimes, when in the mood, he would read portions of his progressing *Tortilla Flat*. One of his eager listeners, up from Eagle Rock, was Dook Sheffield.

A prosperous and pompous out-of-town doctor accompanied a Carmel acquaintance to one of the gatherings. His repeated efforts to steer the conversation to his own professon fell flat. Only one thing was of interest at these gatherings — writing. At last the doctor turned to Steinbeck.

"Some day," he said, "I'm going to take time off and write a book."

John mulled that over briefly, getting madder by the moment. "Some day," he replied, voice rising,"I'm going to take time off, too — and perform an appendectomy."

Occasionally there were visits to New Monterey to see Ed Ricketts. Ricketts was wearing well as a friend and teacher, not only because of his views on ecology but also his philosophy of life, his fascination with music and other arts, his interest in people, and his robust indulgence in life. A mutual interest in marine biology also linked the two men strongly.

John's agents had received and liked the final version of *To a God Unknown*. The news spurred him on; his daily word output at this time was tremendous. But the mechanics of providing themselves with the basic necessities of life during these lean days occupied a certain amount of John's time. Sometimes, for fuel, he and Carol would gather driftwood that had washed up on the beach. And sometimes they went fishing for sea trout, blue cod, perch, or sculpin, which supplied a welcome variation from their usual diet of beans, French bread, and red wine. If they brought their own jug in these Prohibition times, they could get the wine for thirty-five cents a gallon — and sometimes for as little as twenty cents. Once, impersonating a strolling minstrel, John brought home a half-dozen quarts in an old guitar case.

Since farmers and orchardists in the nearby countryside couldn't sell their crops, they gave much away. So the Steinbecks and their equally impoverished friends, armed with gunnysacks, occasionally went on walking tours — and came back loaded with produce. They did only a little stealing.

The luxury of meat was a time for celebration. In *Esquire*'s "Primer on the 30's," Steinbeck recalled "one great meat loaf carried in shoulder high like a medieval boar's head," garnished with paper strips of bacon cut from an advertisement. A big moment came when, in back of

Holman's store, John found a discarded papier-mâché roast turkey that had outlived its usefullness as a window display. However, repaired and varnished at home, the make-believe old gobbler actually looked tempting. John served it on a platter tastefully fringed with dandelions. Under its hollow, counterfeit body reposed a stack of hamburgers.

A frequent visitor at the Steinbeck home was Ted Durien, a reporter covering Pacific Grove for the *Monterey Herald*. The two men would sit on the shady stoop with a brass bowl of Bull Durham between them, and, as they rolled their cigarettes, shoot the breeze about anything and everything, from the day's work to characters in a story.

One day after leaving John, Durien encountered Flora Wood, a madam whose girls were as beautiful and well behaved as any in the trade. Both John and Durien had known her for years.

"Some day," Durien told her by way of a compliment, "John Steinbeck says he'll put you in a book."

"He shouldn't do that," Flora protested. "I always liked John. He shouldn't do it. I'll tell you what," — she brightened — "if John puts me in a book, you write a book about me, and we'll put *John* in it."

But to her subsequent delight, Flora did appear in not only one, but at least two books — as Dora Williams in *Tortilla Flat* and as the generous and efficient Dora Flood in *Cannery Row*, who presided over the Bear Flag — "no fly-by-night cheap clip joint" but "a decent, clean, honest, old-fashioned" whorehouse.

To make it possible for John to devote most of his hours to writing, Carol took a number of jobs. For a time she did secretarial work for the Monterey Chamber of Commerce, then became a library cataloguer for the old S. E. R. A.— State Emergency Relief Administration — and next worked as Ed Rickett's secretary at the Pacific Biological Laboratory. Later she tried running her own free-lance advertising agency, in which she was joined by a Miss Ingels of the *Herald*. The venture didn't pan out well. "We didn't lose any money," Carol says, "but wore out our feet." She was undisturbed by gossips who whispered that her husky husband should be pushing a wheelbarrow instead of a pen. And if she and John fought bitterly at times, mutual friends pictured her as a perfect catalyst in the writer's life.

John's mother had entered the Salinas Valley Hospital, her hypertension growing steadily worse. By this time, despairing of her son's business chances, Olive Steinbeck was pretty much reconciled to his writing career. Regularly she read from his published works on the bedside table and eagerly offered to loan copies to her nurses. Whenever Mary Morley came in, Mrs. Steinbeck would beg her to borrow a volume and read it, which Mary eventually did. Olive also prevailed upon Lena O'Shay, another R.N., to take one of the novels. Not having time to read it, however, Lena hid it under her mattress for safekeeping; then on returning it, still unread, she brightly came out with the comment that she had spent pleasant hours on the book. She never felt guilty about twisting the truth, either. The patient was made happy.

John frequently visited his mother and would always find her propped up in bed awaiting him. Her hair would be nicely fixed and she would be wearing a pretty bed jacket. For his part, John would be dressed disreputably but in about the best clothes he owned — usually worn trousers, old sweat shirt, and invariably a long, floppy overcoat with a side pocket torn away.

He would sit with her for hours, sometimes neither of them saying a word. Occasionally, at her request, he would spend his time scribbling in a note pad, while his mother's eyes would be fixed raptly upon him.

As the end of the year approached, Mrs. Steinbeck, now paralyzed, was permitted to return to her Central Avenue home. Completely bedridden, she was only faintly interested in preparations for the holidays.

"The most terrible wrenching scene I can remember in my life was the Christmas after my mother was paralyzed. My father tried to make an old Christmas. We decorated a tree in her room and had presents and tried to make the Christmas jokes. And I remember her eyes — cold as marbles but alive. I don't know how much she could see or understand. But it breaks me up every time I remember how hard my father tried. It's little wonder he didn't live long after she died." — *Journal of a Novel.*

Olive Steinbeck died at home of a stroke, on February 19, 1934. Shortly before her death, John revealed he had seen a translucent "white column" standing beside her body while gazing intently down upon it. After her death, when he and his father were sitting in the living room, John saw this same column drift slowly into the room, turn, enter the dining room, hover around the china cupboard as his mother used to do, and disappear into the kitchen.

John's novel *Tortilla Flat* had long since been submitted, but was having trouble finding a New York home. Among the publishers to back away from the story was Robert O. Ballou, who had already produced *Pastures of Heaven* (which he still maintains was John's best writing) and *To a God Unknown*, but both had sold poorly. Even though he had a firm contract to print a third Steinbeck book, he wanted no part of this latest novel (one, ironically, that would have turned the tide of fortune in his favor). He didn't much like it. Furthermore, his small publishing business was failing and he faced a mounting indebtedness; for him to turn out the book, he said, would be unfair to them both.

Ballou was only one of five publishers to reject *Tortilla Flat*, all of them failing to recognize the story's theme. In March 1934, exasperated by the readers' reactions in various publishing houses, John wrote his agents that he believed he had made this point clear. Equally important, at least to him, had been his intention to portray an unfamiliar and captivating group of people.

Just one month after the letter to McIntosh and Otis, "The Murder" appeared in the April issue of *North American Review* and was subsequently selected as an O. Henry prize story of 1934. *North American* also ran "The Raid" in October of that year and scheduled "The White Quail" for its March 1935 issue. Previously, in its November and December issues of 1933, it had run the first two parts of *The Red Pony*.

Already deep into a book of an entirely different sort, John spread blood and skull-crunching blows over many a page of a realistic strike novel he was writing in Pacific Grove — a story of labor unrest in Torgas Valley. The formative idea for the story had been what he termed his "phalanx theory," or group-man concept, where the behavior of groups differs from that of individuals thinking and acting separately. He had long pondered mob psychology, had studied labor conditions, and was now giving the subject his best efforts. And although he was unaware of it at the time of course, *In Dubious Battle* eventually would be considered by many critics as one of his fine works (indeed, it was the favorite of biographer Joseph Fontenrose); certainly it would focus attention upon the plight of migratory crop harvesters and the efforts of party organizers to line them up.

Despite his absorption in the new novel, he was preoccupied by family concerns. He grew more and more disturbed over the condition of his father, who, ever since Olive's death, had gone steadily downhill. His eyesight was beginning to fail and feebleness was evident. Arteriosclerosis was the diagnosis. The senior Steinbeck was living by himself in the big house on Central Avenue, which had become a lonely place.

Eventually, a married couple whom he knew moved in to keep him company. He talked but little and, after listening to the nine o'clock evening news, went promptly to bed.

John and Carol came over regularly, doing little chores around the house and helping as best they could. And at day's end, to keep his father from brooding, John would read aloud from a manuscript, just as his father had read to him long ago within those very walls. On these occasions, but only then, Mr. Steinbeck perked up, seeming to become alert and interested.

As February neared an end, Mr. Steinbeck's arteriosclerosis was pronounced acute. He was moved to Watsonville, where his daughter Esther lived. Three months later — on May 23 1935, only five days before his son's *Tortilla Flat* was published — he died of a brain hemorrhage.

In Pacific Grove, during working hours, John stuck closely to his new story, although other writings did appear in print. A friend, Peter O'Crotty, editor of a small, avant-garde magazine called *The Monterey Beacon*, asked for contributions. Steinbeck obliged with several poems signed "Amnesia Glasscock" — possibly, though, the work of Carol — and a short story he had previously written, "A Snake of One's Own," which was published in June. The genesis of that story further illustrates how he converted real life to fiction.

One evening he and Toby Street had gone to the Blue Bell restaurant, whose floor show included a tall, sleepy-eyed blonde from out of town. They told the dancer they wanted her to meet a distinguished Dr. Ricketts after the show.

In the laboratory on Cannery Row, Doc looked the girl over, showing interest, but said there was work to do. It was time, he explained, to feed his charges. Going to a wire cage, he picked out a white rat and dropped it into a glass cage containing two big rattlesnakes. One of the rattlers, after biding its time, sank a fang into this welcome morsel, just behind the ear. For a while the rat frolicked around, then fell over dead. As the reptile swallowed its dinner, headfirst and whole, the girl watched in fascination. Presently she whirled around, grabbed her coat, and ran out the front door. Her hosts never saw her again. From that incident John built his suspenseful story, "The Snake," which, after being printed in *The Beacon* appeared in *The Long Valley* and, as "A Snake of One's Own," in *The Bedside Esquire*, *Great American Short Stories*, and *The Best*, "a continuing anthology of the world's greatest writing."

John often visited the bayside lab with Toby or other mutual friends, watching Doc Ricketts at work over slides and microscope. The walls of the entry were lined with shelves holding mounted marine specimens. In other areas were the rat and snake cages, dissecting tables, and varied paraphernalia used in Ricketts' biological supply business.

When Doc was in the clear, he joined his friends to guzzle beer and discuss women, philosophy, music, science, poetry, whatever came to mind. Sometimes he sat silently with eyes closed, nodding, but hearing everything, an attitude that won him the nickname of "the mandarin." His effect upon John's future writings was immense. Steinbeck would one day say of him, ". . . I knew him better than I knew anyone, and perhaps I did not know him at all."

CHAPTER **NINETEEN**

BEN Abramson was puttering around in the rear of his tunnel-like Chicago bookstore when he raised his eyes to see a man's silhouette up front, surrounded by puffs of cigar smoke. Abramson hurried forward to greet an old friend, Pat Covici.

Pascal Covici did not look the part of a New York publisher in dire financial straits. A handsome man whose black mane of hair was beginning to surrender to an invasion of gray, deliberate in his movements, he appeared like a carefree browser enjoying the afternoon. After a warm reunion and a few chuckles, the pair talked of old times, their families, trade conditions, and, finally, a few business matters.

As the caller prepared to leave, Abramson pointed to a nearby counter of ten-cent bargain books that had been "remaindered" by their hard-hit publisher, Ballou. Was Covici familiar with the author? At a negative reply, the store owner chided him, saying, "I don't see how any intelligent man could have failed to read John Steinbeck." He pressed a copy of *Pastures of Heaven* upon his friend.

On the train going back home, Covici lit a fresh cigar and idly opened the bargain book beside him. Soon he was oblivious to everything else. Next day, scenting a find, he rang McIntosh and Otis, expressing an interest in the California writer. They sent him the draft of *Tortilla Flat*, which a publisher had returned to them that very morning.

Pat Covici spent more than half the night going over the manuscript. At breakfast next morning he excitedly proclaimed: "This man's got it! Great feeling for words! Great power of description and dialogue! Why people didn't like him before, I'll never know."

Those in the office of Covici-Friede were equally impressed. But did they dare embark on this venture? Did they dare pour money into publishing a novel by an author whose previous books had been failures? They knew the manuscript's bad history; they knew that some of bookdom's best men had shied away. Nevertheless, they wavered.

If only they could depend on the critics reading the book, they reasoned, reviews would be favorable. But read it the critics must! Then they hit upon a promising scheme. They would have the work illustrated by Ruth Gannett, a talented artist with the right sense of humor for such a commission — an artist whose husband happened to be the critic Lewis Gannett. They felt that he, for one, would surely weigh a novel assigned to his wife and that his colleagues in respect to him, would do the same.

When *Tortilla Flat* came off the press on May 28, 1935, Covici wanted personally to deliver the first royalty payment — a check for $299.44 issued on the publication date, on accrued sales. McIntosh and Otis applauded the idea. Through correspondence, since he was going west anyway, Covici set a San Francisco hotel lobby as the meeting place.

At the specified time, the publisher was there, watching the lobby entrance. Presently a tall, husky, curly-haired fellow in slightly misfit clothes came in. Covici spotted John Steinbeck instantly. The two men got together, and after a while the New Yorker presented the check. Steinbeck stared at it silently, grinning in satisfaction. Impulsively he invited the donor of the "fortune" to his home for dinner.

Covici accepted. But before the two left for Pacific Grove, John shopped for some cheese, wine, and French bread, plus "a little present" for his wife — a dressing gown. It cost eight dollars.

In the Pacific Grove home, Carol excitedly unwrapped her victory gift, and was ecstatic. After all the hard times and shoddiness and making do, here was something beautiful and wonderful. Only eight dollars? Why it was priceless! Slipping into the garment, she proudly modeled it and pirouetted around the tiny room.

The Covici-Friede plan worked, and worked beautifully. The critics *did* read *Tortilla Flat* — and were delighted. So was the public. The nation took Steinbeck to its heart, which was beginning to beat now that the depression was ebbing a bit, a tiny bit. The book hit the best-seller list and also won the California Commonwealth Club's gold medal for the year's best novel on California.

Naturally Steinbeck was pleased with the medal. There was an ironic aftermath, however, according to his friend, Herb Caen, columnist for the *San Francisco Chronicle*.

Always Steinbeck guarded that gold medal as a good hedge against hard times. If he ever went broke again, as he had done in the early 30s, he could hock it and buy some beans. He wouldn't go hungry anymore.

"Well, I finally took my shiny, yellow prize into a Salinas jewelry store for appraisal," John said. "The jeweler screwed his eyepiece into his eye, squinted hard at it, made some tests, and looked up. 'That's the thinnest gold plate I ever saw,' he told me. 'I wouldn't give you a nickel for it.' "

That first royalty payment was the beginning of better times for John. In November 1935 he was summoned to New York to sign a $4,000 motion picture contract on *Tortilla Flat*. When the signing ceremony was over, John wanted to go shopping in celebration. Elizabeth Otis accompanied him to Macy's and couldn't help being amused by his boyish pleasure in riding the escalators. Then on December 31 the next royalty check was issued. It was for $1,313. Everything was clicking.

Since then, *Tortilla Flat* has been selling strongly in many languages. Its characters have become part of Monterey folklore. There a brawling drunk is a Pilon or a Danny; a man followed by a pack of devoted dogs is the Pirate. Although Monterey's Johnson Street has been rebuilt and its sagging houses are no more, tourists climb the hill for a nostalgic look. Newspaper stories refer to the novel to illustrate this point or that. Feature writers dig into it often. Families living on the little street feel lucky. They can give Tortilla Flat parties.

Yet it wasn't always so. In a letter, Steinbeck said: "When I wrote *Tortilla Flat* . . . the Monterey Chamber of Commerce issued a statement that it was a damned lie and that no such place or people [the *paisanos*] existed. Later, they began running buses to the place where they thought it might be."

Indeed the novel made such a lasting impression that in 1972, at the time of the Apollo 17 mission to the moon, one stretch of the lunar surface would be named "Tortilla Flat," a landmark for the astronauts. Like "Shakespeare Crater," "Camelot Crater," and other geographic features more than 225,000 miles away, the Steinbeck place name promises to be around for a long, long time.

Before the publication of *Tortilla Flat*, the Pacific Grove house had enjoyed almost monastic quiet, ideal for the flow of dreams and words. Save for the few Carmel friends who trudged over the hill for refreshment and shoptalk, callers had been rare. But the birth of a best seller

156

changed all that. Now the seekers of literary lions, tracking new prey, poured in from everywhere and at every hour. Those not content with oh-h-ing and ah-h-ing outside the tiny cottage, or snorting contemptuously, would insist on interviews, which John loathed. The first sweet smell of success suddenly lost its sweetness. For a while, John tried to put up with the huntsmen, then became infuriated.

As though the intruders weren't trouble enough, upsetting word came from New York. An editor for Covici-Friede, acting on his own, wrote a long and critical report on the manuscript of *In Dubious Battle* questioning the novel's communist ideology and suggesting changes, which John refused to make. The far-left editor felt that Steinbeck was not following the party line satisfactorily. John contended that the challenged views "came mostly from Irish and Italian Communists in the field, not the drawing room," and demanded return of the story. Covici, learning what his editor had done, was aghast. He hastily assured Steinbeck that he wanted to publish the book. Meanwhile, both Bobbs-Merrill and Macmillan had become interested, resulting in a three-way dispute that was settled only when Miss Otis returned from abroad. Ultimately, in January 1936, the book was brought out by Covici-Friede. The novel excited both praise and condemnation, built John's status in the labor field, sold well, and won another Commonwealth gold medal.

But in Pacific Grove, conditions had become intolerable. John and Carol finally threw up their hands in despair. They'd have to run away. After some exploring, they found an appealing home site in rolling hills, about fifty miles north of the Monterey Peninsula. Carol did most of the planning of the new house, which was built on a sloping acre, a mile or two west of Los Gatos. Peace and quiet seemed assured. The board-and-batten structure sat well back from winding Greenwood Lane and was about fifty feet below it. An eight-foot unenclosed porch on the south side overlooked the canyon below. John's study was at the far end of the house where he could work undisturbed, and an eight-foot grapestake fence was erected just off the road, for the sake of continued privacy.

Despite all precautions, however, interruptions began again. John decided to get away for a while. Now he could afford that long-delayed trip to Mexico. In the autumn he and Carol left in a battered secondhand car, but were back before year's end.

Now the intruders really descended in earnest. They came for autographs, advice on writing, and sometimes just to get acquainted. A few, apparently assuming that every writer had Hollywood connections, even sought aid in crashing filmland. A lock was put on the gate. Intruders broke the lock.

One day a bedraggled woman and her daughter, about eight, mysteriously showed up in the front yard where John was getting a breath of air. The little girl's nose was running, her knees were skinned and grimy, her clothing torn. Shoving her offspring forward, the woman shrilly insisted that her child was a natural-born movie star. John's protests went unheeded.

"Dance for the man, Mildred!" the woman commanded. "Dance!"

Mildred danced — on tiptoe, all around the yard. She also stumbled and fell, but regained her feet to bow awkwardly before departing — without a movie contract in her pocket.

In a last-ditch effort to discourage interruptions, John tore down the legend "Steinbeckia," substituting another which said, *Arroya del Ajo*," but even "Garlic Gulch" failed to sidetrack the public. Then new houses started springing up, the clatter of unloading lumber and the thudding of hammers assaulting the air. Peering neighbors were the last straw. On one such occasion, to get even with a staring neighboring housewife, John strode onto his porch; then, making sure he was seen, unbuttoned his pants and sent an amber stream arcing over the side. The woman fled in horror.

"Six houses went up all about us and it was like living in an apartment house," he wrote. "Besides, the land was too expensive. It grew to be three thousand dollars an acre and you couldn't grow a radish on it."

Despite the myriad frustrations on Greenwood Lane, Steinbeck was mulling over an exciting idea for a new story, another novel on itinerant ranch workers but totally unlike anything he'd ever done. A Salinas Valley ranch would furnish the locale. And he personally knew, or had observed, the characters he'd use, one of whom was the "ape man" of Castroville from his boyhood days.

Intrigued by the thought of writing a play, he hoped to do a story which he would call "a novel to be played," one that could be lifted, almost intact, from the printed page to the stage. Dialogue would be typical bunkhouse talk, scenic background would be held to a minimum. Soon he fell to work on "Something That Happened," a title later changed to *Of Mice and Men*. Two months' work had gone into it when his setter pup, Toby, left alone one night, ripped into the manuscript, turning much of it into confetti. He rewrote.

In May 1937, *Of Mice and Men* had its national premiere at the Green Street Playhouse in San Francisco under the auspices of the San Francisco Theater Union. Newspaper critics saw the stage portrayal of the two lonely and inarticulate ranch hands as poignant and fairly effective. The play was well received but certainly not wildly acclaimed. Obviously doctoring was needed.

That same spring, now financially able to travel, the Steinbecks took a freighter to New York, via the Panama Canal, where John visited his agents, squirmed into a borrowed suit to attend a dinner party, and signed a contract for the filming of *Of Mice and Men*. A European trip followed, and the Steinbecks were back in New York again by early August. John immediately went to work with George S. Kaufmann on a project delayed by the European jaunt — a dramatization of *Of Mice and Men*. At Kaufmann's farm in Bucks County, Pennsylvania, the noted playwright turned adviser and consultant, expressing his enthusiasm for the way the novel lent itself to the stage.

"Kaufmann would be reading over the lines to me and suddenly he'd stop," Steinbeck said later. "He can tell ahead of time just when an audience is going to suppress a titter or when it will burst into a belly-laugh or when it will remain completely silent. The man's a marvel." While Kaufmann didn't write a line of the dialogue, his suggestions were invaluable.

Finishing the play, and after helping interview eighty applicants for the roles of Lennie and George but without waiting for opening night, John wearily headed for the West Coast, anxious to get home and start another farmland story, then in its planning and early writing stages. Contrary to long-perpetuated myths, he did not tarry to join the Okies and Arkies on their migration westward.

Did he ever worry how New York would accept his *Mice* drama? At about six o'clock on the evening of November 23, 1937, he admitted, he felt his stomach slowly turning around as he realized the curtain had just risen on the first act at New York's Music Box Theatre. There was no reason to worry. Audiences cried openly and beat their hands deafeningly. Critics were enraptured. The play ran through April, when it was awarded the New York Drama Critics' silver plaque as the best American play to be produced in a New York theatre during the 1937-38 season.

Interviewed at his home, Steinbeck denied there were any subtle implications in the play. "All I tried to write was the story of two Salinas

Valley vagrants," he said. "It hasn't any meaning or special significance outside of what appears on the surface. It's just a story. I don't know what it means, if anything, and damned if I care. My business is only storytelling."

CHAPTER TWENTY

AT the core of John's eagerness to get back to California was a writing project which he had started before *Of Mice and Men* and was now anxious to complete. Set in the rich agricultural valleys in the interior of California, the novel would expose the appalling conditions endured by the farm workers. John's interest in the subject was nothing new. In his earlier book, *In Dubious Battle*, he had also focused attention on farm labor's unrest in California. Largely because of the reputation he had made through that novel, in 1936 the *San Francisco News* had asked him if he would write a series of articles exposing conditions in rural areas. Steinbeck needed no prodding to accept the assignment. And thus was planted the seed that would become his best-known work, *The Grapes of Wrath*.

As he began the *News* assignment, Steinbeck already knew that the ranks of customary field workers — Mexicans, Filipinos, Japanese, and Chinese — had been enormously increased by the addition of dust bowl refugees, migrants who had been evicted from their drought-stricken lands in the Midwest, primarily in Oklahoma and Arkansas. Working in these fields, orchards, and vineyards, many lived in Hoovervilles — ramshackle squatters' camps they had put together for themselves. But what disturbed Steinbeck most were reports that the big agricultural interests were taking unfair advantage of the labor surplus, working the Okies and Arkies longer and longer hours for less and less money, causing untold hardship. He decided to go see for himself.

Heading down the San Joaquin Valley, he mingled with the workers, looked and listened. Observation turned to outrage. The destitute migrants had but one obsession — to make what money they could before the crop was harvested and it was time to move along to other crops just coming in, sometimes a hundred miles away. Competition for jobs was fierce, giving the employers just the opportunity they wanted.

Bitterness burned in the eyes of the workers. Their faces were sullen and frightened. Many families, Steinbeck found, were sinking deeper and deeper into debt as they tried vainly to get out of the quagmire.

John talked with the father in a family of six who lived in a small tent swarming with flies, which alighted on the apple crate that served as their dinner table. The meals of fried dough, fried cornmeal, and beans were cheap but filling — and inadequate. The mother's breasts were without milk for the baby. Only recently a fifth child had been carried away in the coroner's wagon.

John offered one woman a cigarette. She took several puffs and vomited in his presence. Apologizing, she said smoke made her sick because she hadn't eaten in two days.

He talked to a man who tried to explain why his little girl couldn't go to school. She was too weak to walk there.

The typical squatters' camp he visited looked from a distance like a city dump. "Homes" were built of anything and everything — scrap metal, flattened cans, gunnysacks, and corrugated paper, all attached to willow branches and wattling weeds driven into the ground.

Steinbeck also learned of the methods used by the farm operators. When the owners of small 500- to 600-acre farms needed seasonal workers, they usually drew from the squatters' camps. While they tried to pay fair wages, they were held in line by the large operators and the mortgage-holding banks. The large farms often operated their own camps for the workers, providing miserable houses for which they charged rent.

A fairly typical ranch in Kern County had row upon row of houses, with a single cold-water shower serving 400 people. Deputized employees, with guns conspicuous, policed the area; guards were at the gates; roads were patrolled. Crowds were not allowed to gather; it was feared they might organize. Troublemakers were forced out at gunpoint.

It was in Weedpatch, a model government camp near Bakersfield, that he met the one person most important to his survey — Tom Collins, a psychologist and government employee, understanding and compassionate. He managed the camp for the Farm Security Administration. Collins knew the Okies and their problems intimately — and provided invaluable information. In the camp's welcome surroundings, the migrants talked freely, fearing no retaliation. In lieu of rent, they paid for their neat living quarters by devoting two hours a week toward maintenance and improvement of the camp. Food sold at reasonable prices, and little plots of ground were provided each family, where in off hours, they could raise their own vegetables. A measure of dignity and decency returned to those lucky enough to qualify for this patch of heaven.

The Steinbeck articles, called "The Harvest Gypsies," ran serially in the *San Francisco News* (October 1936) and were later published in pamphlet form as "Their Blood is Strong," by the Simon J. Lubin Society of California (1938).

They proved to be an eye-opening sensation — but, unfortunately were soon forgotten. It was left to the future, powerful *Grapes of Wrath* to help launch the push toward long-overdue reform.

However, *Grapes of Wrath* was not John's first attempt to fashion a novel out of his survey for the *News*. The book he came home from New York to work on was titled *L'Affaire Lettuceberg*. Soon after he finished, he changed his mind about wanting it published, even though it had already been announced. In a joint letter to his publisher and his agents, he termed the work "bad," the kind of thing his father would have called "a smart-aleck" book, and moreover he said it was badly written. He didn't want it printed and added that he wasn't ready to become a hack yet. Abjectly he apologized for his decision and announced his plan to work on another book, the yet unnamed *Grapes of Wrath*.

Dook Sheffield was one of the first to see sections of the work in progress. In the big living room on Greenwood Lane, John brought out a sheaf of manuscript to read to his friend. Pacing before the copper-hooded fireplace, he read the *Grapes'* realistic description of the symbolic land turtle — a passage that in a future day would often be included in freshman English texts. Dook was impressed.

After contending for three years with the endless intruders and other invasions of privacy at Greenwood Lane, the Steinbecks were finally able to leave the place, thanks to Carol's father. He had found them a "dream ranch" further up the mountain, five miles from Los Gatos. It seemed an ideal hideaway.

Off winding Hebard Road, the old 47-acre Biddle ranch had been continuously occupied since 1850. It had its own water resources, a small forest, an orchard, vineyard, pasture, scattered oaks, firs, and madrones; even an abandoned oil well with an echo. Talk into it, and pretty soon your words would come booming back from the center of the earth.

John and Carol lived in an old farmhouse on the place while their contractor built them a new home, using many of the fine weathered timbers and boards from the oil-well complex. Rooms were made larger than in their Greenwood place, and the new house commanded a sweeping view of the Santa Clara farmlands. Colorful and comfortable furniture was installed, and Carol hung Mexican tapestries and prints. A long, narrow, sky-blue swimming pool was built and filled with water piped from their own spring-fed lake.

Since John's previous dog had run away, and unable to be without canine company for long, he bought a Doberman Pinscher pup, which they named Bruga.

But his principal occupation, preoccupation and obsession during this period was living and writing his story. Little else mattered. The Steinbecks had an unlisted phone and took no papers. They were literally lost souls — and wanted it that way. As John developed his 200,000-word novel, turning out 2,000 and more words a day, Carol was busy transcribing, which she painstakingly did three times to take care of the revisions. Her difficulty in deciphering some of her husband's tiny script, though, led to some jokes between them. Once quoting Ma Joad, John had written, "He was jes' too big for his overhalls," but when it came out of Carol's typewriter, the sentence read, "He was jes' too big for his own balls." John chortled over that one and was tempted to let the error stand, but didn't. He made use of some material from "The Harvest Gypsies" for the interchapters and dedicated the book to Carol and Tom Collins.

In September 1938 a postcard carried his title for the book to New York, and on a day that autumn *The Grapes of Wrath* was finished.

John and Carol finally took the time for some needed rest and relaxation. Chores were held to a minimum. A Japanese boy was hired to help cook and garden and to look after the place when the Steinbecks were away. Coming out of their self-imposed isolation, they entertained old friends, such as Dook and Doc Ricketts, as well as newer acquaintances. Among the latter was Charlie Chaplin, certainly testimony enough that John was now a certified literary lion. The famous movie comedian, who had just parted from his third wife, Paulette Goddard, pleaded that he be allowed to come back, dismiss the servants, and "just talk about how lonely and sad I am." He insisted he wanted to do it. "He is a good little man," John wrote Dook. "And he knows so much better than I do the horrors of being a celebrity."

Meanwhile, Covici-Friede had been declared bankrupt, and Pascal Covici had gone over to Viking Press as an editor, a lasting affiliation for both himself and Steinbeck. As for *Grapes*, John expressed doubt that his "slow-plodding" book would be popular. He was in for a big surprise.

When Viking published it in April 1939, the book became a runaway best seller. In comparison, it made his earlier successful works — *Tortilla Flat, In Dubious Battle,* and *Of Mice and Men* — look like laggards indeed. Times were right for the new book. The Dust Bowl problems filled the public mind. Here was a story that dramatically and skillfully presented the plight of the homeless Okies. However, opinions on its worth were divided. The plain-spoken story was banned and burned, called obscene, branded a pack of lies — and hailed as the finest literary work in many years.

By mid-May of '39, three months after the publication, more than 83,000 copies had reached the market, and sales kept climbing. Six months later, more than 11,000 copies were selling weekly. The novel headed the best-seller list of 1939 and continued as one of the ten best sellers the following year.

Motion-picture rights to the story were sold to Darryl Zanuck of Twentieth Century-Fox for $75,000. The film had its world premiere at the Rivoli Theatre in New York on January 24, 1940, receiving overwhelming endorsements from the critics and drawing tremendous crowds.

Reviews of the book, for the most part, were laudatory. Joseph Henry Jackson, book critic of the *San Francisco Chronicle* and perhaps the closest follower of the Steinbeck trend, was almost rhapsodic. He said, ". . . [Grapes of Wrath] is the whole Steinbeck, the mature novelist saying something he must say and doing it with the sure touch of the great artist." A national boost came when Mrs. Eleanor Roosevelt chatted about it in her "My Day" column. Reading it, she said, was an "unforgettable experience."

How did John Steinbeck feel about such a response? There's no denying that he appreciated recognition, but what pleased him most of all, far beyond the critical praises, was one simple fact — people were reading him! On the occasion of another honor, years later, he put his feelings into words:

"I had a letter a few weeks ago from a bookseller in one of the outlying districts of Denmark who said, 'I feel you ought to know this. A woman rowed in an open boat over eight miles to bring two chickens to my store to exchange for one of your paperback books.' Just think! Rowing eight miles there and eight miles back — sixteen miles — to trade for one of your books! This is what you write for. This is as good a prize as you can get." — Stockholm Interview.

John was not so fortunate with all his readers. Like most controversial figures, he attracted a screwball fringe whose letters after *Grapes of Wrath* hammered at him mercilessly. Nearly all wanted something, if no more than his time. They interrupted his longed-for privacy, interfered with his sleep, his eating habits, his peace of mind — the very factors that had driven him from the Greenwood Lane home.

His annoyance was expressed in letters to Dook: "I got home about three days ago for a little while and found about five hundred letters that had to be answered. So I have been answering them as quickly as possible. . . . Leisure is a thing I have almost lost track of. . . . The heat is on me and now really going strong. Everybody in North America wants something from me. Remember when I used to like mail so much that I even tried to get on sucker lists? Well, I wish them days back." And, "I have been desperately worried by the pressures which have been put upon me. Success is the most stultifying thing in the world."

Condemnation of *Grapes of Wrath* took various forms. Hatred and resentment swept Salinas. Criticism came from widely scattered sources, including some areas of the Dust Bowl itself. In East St. Louis, Illinois, where a prominent clubwoman pronounced the novel "vile all the way through," the library board ordered the book burned. In Kansas City, a woman member of the Board of Education abhorred the novel's portrayal of "women living like cattle in a shed" and was particularly offended by the stillborn birth in a boxcar — "It portrays life in such a bestial way." Another member of the same board said he had turned against the book when a "wayward" preacher came into the library and had nerve enough to say that a valuable lesson could be learned from *Grapes of Wrath.* The educator added, "I would like to take that book and read it to that minister's congregation. I'll bet he would have been run out of town next day. Such an obscene, indecent book. . . ." But the morals of the library patrons were saved. The book was ordered from the shelves.

In the author's native California, the labor movement accused much of the press of slanting news in favor of the state's big agricultural interests. In response, Hearst papers, such as the *San Francisco Examiner*, had a field day, getting in a few licks at Steinbeck in the bargain in an article printed on August 22, 1939:

"Distinguished and loyal Californians dipped the cloth to wipe some mud off the face of their state.

"The men and women who really know California broadcast facts in indignant answer to recent destructive fiction that has painted a lurid picture of their homeland."

At a luncheon meeting in the Palace Hotel, H.C. Merritt, Jr., a Tulare rancher, sounded the keynote of this collective reply to such fiction on California's serious migrant problem as John Steinbeck's "Grapes of Wrath" and Carey McWilliams' "Factories in the Field":

"These men seek to find the exception to the rule, and make their characters, by inference, the rule."

Ruth Comfort Mitchell, novelist and ranch wife, was another vocal critic. "The California farmer has been pictured as an old Scrooge or a Simon Legree. . . . We deplore the revolutionary leanings of the people who have painted it so." The national president of Pro-America, which sponsored the Palace meeting, told of visiting a ranch where she found "clean tents with floors," "immaculate white houses," and "excellent" medical treatment for the transient farmhands — a picture in complete contradiction to Steinbeck's findings. Harold Pomeroy, executive secretary of the Associated Farmers, called *Grapes of Wrath,* "a destructive, futile book which carries through it a theme of hate. . . ."

Unfavorable opinions were all right with John; he could take them or ignore them. He was used to it. At another time he would characterize criticism as an "ill-tempered parlour game in which nobody gets kissed." But what infuriated him were the *tactics* of the Associated Farmers. Because *Grapes of Wrath* had put them in an unfavorable light, he said they would stop at nothing to discredit him. His bitterness was revealed in a letter to Dook on June 6, 1939:

"Yes, the Associated Farmers have tried to make me retract things by very sly methods. Unfortunately for them the things are thoroughly documented and the materials turned over to the LaFollette Committee and when it was killed by pressure groups all evidence went to the Attorney General. So when they write and ask for proof, I simply ask them to ask the Senate to hold open hearings of the Civil Liberties Committee and they will get immediate documentary proof of my statements although some of them may go to jail as a result of it. And you have no idea how quickly that stops the argument. They can't shoot me now because it would be too obvious and because I have placed certain information in the hands of J. Edgar Hoover in case I take a nose dive. So I think I am personally safe enough except for automobile accidents, etc., and rape and stuff like that, so I am a little careful not to go anywhere alone nor to do anything without witnesses. Seems silly, but I have been carefully instructed by people who know the ropes. So they have gone to the whispering campaign (how in hell do you spell that?) but unfortunately that method only sells more books. I'm due to topple within the next two years but I have that little time left to me. And in many ways I'll be glad when the turn of the thing comes. As it must inevitably."

But fame and more honors stalked John far into the future, although animosities never did die out completely. On May 6, 1940, the Pulitzer Prize for the year's most distinguished novel went to *Grapes of Wrath*, and in 1948 Steinbeck was elected to the National Institute of Arts and Letters.

CHAPTER TWENTY-ONE

STRONGER than a developing fear of crowds was John's restlessness, coupled with a desire to learn more about the making of motion pictures. He went to New York, Washington, and down south — "to see what I can see and hear." Then in Chicago at the invitation of the U.S. Film Service, and under the friendly guidance of Peter Lorenz, he worked in whatever movie-making capacity he could, from carrying lights to helping in the cutting room; he felt that such groundwork might be useful in future script writing. But that experience was not enough. He wanted knowledge of sound equipment, too, and was told the place for that study was Hollywood.

During the summer of 1939, when *The Grapes of Wrath* was going strong, he had a spat with Carol in the movie capital and moved alone into Hollywood's Aloha Apartments — but with a crippling attack of sciatica. Getting out of bed was difficult, lying down still harder, sitting up almost impossible. The slightest turn or twist would start up the throbbing in his hip.

In his apartment he installed a self-operated diathermy machine, its source unknown. Visitors were awed and often amused by the mysterious black box, whose dials and glowing lights, levers and electrodes made it look like something dreamed up by Rube Goldberg. Nevertheless, John used it faithfully and accepted good-naturedly the kidding about his portable contraption, insisting that its magical rays were helping him. One of his frequent visitors was his boyhood friend from Salinas, Max Wagner, now a movie actor. On one of his calls Max asked if John wouldn't like some feminine companionship, such as a singer he knew, who was lively, shapely, blondish, and lots of fun. John never needed much coaxing.

"Her name is Gwyn Conger," Max said.

On a subsequent visit, Max had the pretty young woman in tow. She and John hit it off from the start. Gwyndolyn sympathized with her host, fussed over him, and left a trail of subtle perfume through the apartment. Both she and Max thought a little fresh air and sunshine might do Steinbeck some good.

Whatever the reason — the diathermy machine, the outdoors, or a new interest — John's condition soon improved. He made at least one — and maybe more — trips with Max and Gwyn up Laurel Canyon to see Gwyn's arranger named Sandy Oliver.

Later John and Max visited Brittingham's cocktail lounge, run in connection with Brittingham's restaurant at Gower and Sunset, where an entrancing-looking Gwyn would be singing beside the piano in the soft radiance of a spotlight. Now and then her glance would drift to the two men, and between numbers she would join them at their table. She talked with a pleasing, well-practiced voice. And sometimes she produced from nowhere a pet white mouse which she carefully placed on her lovely shoulder. The rodent remained there patiently, twitching its nose as it watched the guests through beady, pink eyes.

Before long, John thought he had better be getting back to Los Gatos and his wife — which was in no way a sign that he and Gwyn had closed the book on their friendship.

John's old unpredictability was driven forcefully home to George Mors, who now lived in Los Gatos.

Before sunrise one day, John's old Stanford roommate showed up at the Hebard Road place and was surprised to find it in total darkness. Previously, he and John had agreed to go quail hunting on this day, the last day of the season. They had even shaken hands on it, John eagerly saying he must remember to get a hunting license ahead of time. Yet now, on the appointed hour, there was no sign of activity in the Steinbeck home. Mors pounded on the door.

Carol answered in her wrapper. "What the hell do you want?" she demanded. "It's five o'clock!"

"I know. John and I have a date to go quail hunting."

"He's not up."

"Well, get him up."

She seemed reluctant to try alone, so both went into the bedroom together, where John was snuggled under the covers. "I'm not going!" he mumbled.

"But why?" Mors pressed.

After a brief hesitation, John drawled sleepily, "I've thought it over. Why should I spend two dollars for a license when there's only one day of hunting left?"

"But we've got a date! You said to be here early."

"Not going!"

George was not surprised at this about-face. He knew John's nature. What did surprise him, however, was the seeming penny-pinching. However, he concedes that miserliness may not have been John's real reason; maybe he just wanted to sleep late, a theory supported the following day when John bought *two* new automobiles — one for Carol and one for himself! "Wouldn't spend two bucks for hunting but bounced for a pair of cars — Packards or Cads, at that — hoo-*ee!*"

So George went hunting alone — and didn't get one damned shot.

In nearly every letter to Dook during this period, John still betrayed concern over the results of success and the demands made upon him. Just as he had written his agents earlier that he was increasingly afraid in crowds, he now wrote Sheffield in the same vein, adding, "Knowing I'm watched, I don't go any place. Knowing I'll be quoted, I don't say anything. In other words, I'm slightly shell-shocked." As for mail, he said, "I'm sure getting it now in bales and very little of it pleasant."

And later: "I've seen some of the private reports of the [LaFollette] committee. It is amazing how some of our best citizens will take up murder. . . . You should hear some of the threats against me. They are melodramatic. The best was from a man who said I would never get out of this world alive. Be a good thing if I could."

It was ironic that his long-sought success should, at least in his opinion, almost prove his undoing. His dread of public attention was based on more than simple reticence; he feared its effect would be shattering to his naturalness as a writer. Keenly he believed what he had written to the librarian Lawrence Clark Powell, ". . . a single best-seller can ruin a writer forever," and that he must avoid at all cost an excess of self-consciousness.

In 1939 John was spending considerable time at the Pacific Biological Laboratories, as was Carol, a change in John's living pattern that had come about gradually and for a variety of reasons. Certainly his friendship for Ed Ricketts and his growing interest in marine biology had played a part, and, quite likely he was eager to escape the attention now directed at his home in the hills. By the end of the year he was spending nearly all his weekdays in the lab, studying and doing some independent research.

Under the careless management of Ricketts, who was interested more in natural science for its own sake and in the pleasures of living, the laboratories fell deeply into debt. John bailed out the business and accepted corporation stock, thus becoming, in a sense, Ricketts' partner, which gave the firm as unlikely a team of "head men" as can be imagined.

One of their early projects was to plan an expedition into the Gulf of California to collect marine specimens and make a survey of invertebrates. They chartered a 76-foot purse seiner, the *Western Flyer*, and, after provisioning her amply, pulled out of Monterey on March 11, 1940. Aboard, in addition to Ricketts, John, and Carol, was a crew of four. Carol, who had signed on as cook, went strangely unmentioned in the resulting book, *The Log from the Sea of Cortez*. Webster (Toby) Street accompanied them as far as San Diego, where on a brief stop they were visited by newsmen. Steinbeck mumbled that the trip was a "sort of study into animal sociology." Then he added, "I don't pretend to know much about biology, but it seems that some of the broader, more general aspects of the tie-in of all animal species with one another has been lost since Darwin went out of the picture. We are trying in our small way to get back to a phase of that broader view."

Pressed further, he explained that they were looking especially for marine invertebrates — starfish, crustaceans, worms, and the like — but that their main interest lay in the communities of these animals: how they got along together, the interrelationship of the species that live between the gulf tides. When the trip was over, he said, he planned to write a new book in collaboration with Ricketts — an account of the expedition, with all their scientific findings included in a form valuable to the scientist and interesting to the layman.

Once under way, the expedition became an exhilarating adventure, an odyssey of hard work, study, and play. Carol slept in a forward cabin, John with the crew farther back. Carol and Sparky Enea, a mate, did the cooking. John helped wash and dry the dishes. While pertinent details were recounted in the resulting book, certain other matters were not.

All hands kept alert for seafood delicacies, which they enjoyed often.

They also took aboard between 500 and 1,000 tidal fauna, as well as countless curios for relatives and friends. Already, a decision had been made on how they would approach the book. John would write the first part, a narrative of the trip, and Ricketts would handle the second section, a phyletic catalogue. They would work closely, leaning heavily upon one another.

Occasionally, on pleasant evenings, there would be impromptu entertainment on deck, where John would play the piccolo (ten-cent store variety), and Carol would work a harmonica, while the crew sang. No one ever got bored. One afternoon, after some imbibing, Sparky swam around the boat. It seemed like a good idea. So Carol jumped overboard fully clothed, an incident witnessed by people on three nearby yachts. Soon a report was circulated that a "terrible fight" had been waged and a woman hurled into the sea.

Hitler's rampaging in Europe, snatches of which they learned from other boats, was disturbing — and right when they hoped to remain completely away from world contacts! One militant encounter of their own — but with a refreshing lighter side — occurred one afternoon when they were all ashore in Guaymas.

In a cantina, over a tequila, Steinbeck casually mentioned that one of his crew, the deckhand, had been a bantamweight champ of the Navy in 1931, which was true. A fast-talking promoter nearby told of a fight to be held in Guaymas that very evening. So it was that Ratzi (Tiny) Colletto was booked on the spot to meet "Kid Señorita," whose effeminate-sounding name pleased Tiny very much. "I'll murder him!" Tiny boasted. "Atta boy," John put in. "They don't scare us, do they?"

Tiny was less cocky when he met his opponent shortly before the fight. Kid Señorita was a ferocious-looking character who weighed 174 pounds. Dozens of clippings told of the Kid's knockout victories. Tiny's shipmates tried to call off the match. They couldn't. The four-round bout had waggishly been billed as an "exhibition." Sparky Enea would be Tiny's second.

For the first two rounds, 124-pound Tiny did well, and then the cognac on which he had been training all afternoon began to tell. Further, the ring was sloping, giving his all-wise opponent a downhill advantage. Smash to the eye, cross to the chin, it was slambang all the way. The four hundred spectators screamed for more blood. Finally, in the fourth round, Tiny was hanging on the ropes; another blow sent him to the canvas. Sparky looked desperately for a towel, then ran over to the Kid's corner and threw in that one. Next, he dashed to help his fighter up, but Tiny merely rolled over and kept mumbling thickly, "Jus' let me sleep."

On learning that their man was not seriously hurt, Steinbeck and the crew had their heartiest laugh of the expedition and never let Tiny forget that he had been rocked into slumberland by a "señorita."

Some of Steinbeck's word pictures in *The Log from the Sea of Cortez* haunt the mind long after the reading. Of the homeward trip, he nostalgically wrote, "The *Western Flyer* hunched into the great waves toward Cedros Island, the wind blew off the tops of the whitecaps, and the big guy wire, from bow to mast, took up the vibration like the low pipe of a tremendous organ. It sang its deep note into the wind."

When the *Western Flyer* pulled into its home port of Monterey on April 20, after an absence of nearly six weeks, a welcoming crowd lined the pier. Long before this noisy reception, however, many details of the expedition had already become known, thanks to periodic news notes from Sparky, sent by mail to the *Monterey Herald* but claimed to have been flown in by Stumpy, a legendary, dissolute, one-legged seagull. More than once, after the trip, all the crew gathered at the Steinbeck ranch to reminisce, and Tiny Colletto would invariably be asked for a speech on the finer arts of boxing. He wouldn't talk.

Steinbeck fretted to begin writing the *Sea of Cortez,* but other matters demanded immediate attention. Soon he was on the move again, this time in an old bakery truck with panel body, headed for Mexico City and vicinity, where he briefly helped produce a movie he had written, *The Forgotten Village.* Then, in Hollywood, he acted in an advisory capacity on some final details of the picture.

He went to the film capital, in fact, whenever he could, associating with various actors, directors, and others making movies. Whether he ever saw Gwyn on these trips is not on record, but in the light of future developments, one cannot but wonder. Certainly she was much on his mind. Meanwhile, tiffs with Carol were becoming more frequent.

Early in 1941 he finally barreled into the *Cortez* project, which was a drastic turnaround from his days at Stanford when he had sought to learn more about people, even if it meant studying cadavers in a pre-med course. And it was a fresh adventure in writing, for heretofore, of course, his greatest successes had been based upon depiction of mankind, not fish.

Cortez was finally published in December of '41, the month the United States entered World War II. That Steinbeck enjoyed this writing project as much as any he had ever tackled is evident from even the most cursory reading. Deep feeling is there, and an uninterrupted lilt, whether he is speaking of scientific matters or nights in cantinas. In perhaps no other work has so much of himself come through, including his growing biological interests (thanks to Ricketts), his non-teleological thinking, a good deal of his philosophy, his and Ricketts' ecological concern, his speculation upon what Lisca terms "the mystic unity of all life," his ingrained compassion, and his refreshing sense of humor.

During this period John's restlessness sent him into the sky; he took flying lessons at the Palo Alto airport, saying he hoped to learn the controls while his reflexes were still malleable. In a letter he expressed his love for flying: "There's something so . . . remote and beautiful and detached about being way to hell and gone up on a little yellow leaf . . . there's no sense of power at all but rather a sense of being alone in the best sense of the word, not loneliness at all but just an escape into something delightful. I think you used to get it after you had had a lot of guests and they all went home and the house was finally cleaned up and you could turn on the radio and cook your own kind of stew and look up and know god damned well that you were alone. . . ."

Marital life was not running smoothly. When John wasn't in Pacific Grove, he was in Hollywood. By June of 1941, Carol was living in New York. The rift in the marriage was serious indeed, which did not surprise intimate friends. Altercations were nothing new to their relationship — they had been fighting since their wedding day — but in the past they had been able to work through their misunderstandings. Carol was still willing; not so, John.

In a New York press interview Carol was quoted as saying that "she was fighting for her man." "I suppose every married couple faces a situation like this," she reportedly told Helen Worden, who was on assignment for Scripps-Howard Service. Carol wanted her husband back. "If we wait, perhaps John and I will be better and . . . finer for it. I know our love won't be the same. There won't be the blind devotion, the dumb trust, but there will be a new understanding . . ."

In New York Carol was trying to make it on her own by modeling small, humorous ceramic figures. She could have sold her work if she'd signed it "Mrs. John Steinbeck," which she said she'd be damned if she'd do. "Now, none of this noble-little-woman stuff," she reportedly told her interviewer. "That isn't me. I'm trying to be understanding. It's damned hard."

By the time Carol returned to the West Coast, she had given up all hope of reconciliation and sued for divorce. The action was tried in the superior court in Salinas, Carol testifying briefly that she had been left alone too much of the time and blaming John's absences on "other women" — particularly one in Hollywood. Carol was represented by Attorney Webster Street of Monterey, John's close friend over the years. John did not appear at the courthouse, but asked the court through a written agreement to approve a property settlement by which

Carol would receive about $220,000. The marriage of twelve years was dissolved by Superior Judge H.G. Jorgensen in little more than six minutes.

CHAPTER TWENTY-TWO

DESPITE his hatred for war, Steinbeck was swept by the same patriotic fervor that hit most Americans during World War II, and he was anxious to serve in some way.

A few months after the United States entered the war, in March 1942, *The Moon is Down* was published, his second experiment in the play-novelette form. The book met with some success in the United States, but won great acclaim abroad. With this project out of the way, and in-between more forays to Hollywood, John combined forces with Ed Ricketts to work on a few schemes to help the war effort. They tapped information once prepared by Japanese biologists on the nature of waters around Japanese-held islands in the South Pacific — data concerning currents, reefs, and so on, which they thought might prove valuable if the United States ever attempted beach landings. However, their findings apparently got bogged down in governmental red tape. Another of their ideas, later used successfully by Hitler, was to plant counterfeit money in enemy lands and thereby bring on fiscal chaos. This suggestion was also never acted upon.

As it turned out, his pen provided perhaps his greatest contribution to the war effort. Proposals made by General "Hap" Arnold of the Army Air Force led to the writing of *Bombs Away*, for which John gathered material in trips to various bases with John Swope, photographer and flyer. Hollywood bought the story for $250,000, Steinbeck giving all royalties to the Air Forces Aid society.

One absence from the state found him in New Orleans on March 29, 1943. On that date he and Gwyndolyn Conger were married in the patio of the French quarter home of Lyle Saxon, Louisiana author, with Judge Val J. Stentz of First City Court officiating. From there the newlyweds went to New York, a city John had dreamed about ever since boyhood — ever since he had glimpsed dinky Salinas from atop the Graves' water tower and had made exciting trips with his mother to San

Francisco, when he had vowed some day to live in a big city. (His very first visit to New York, he realized, had hardly made favorable impressions on him, owing to his poverty.)

But even in New York, John was restless. War fever was in his veins, and he promptly accepted an assignment from the *New York Herald Tribune* to report on the G.I.s under fire — an experience that, after more than six months abroad, left him with severe eardrum damage from naval gunfire off the coast of Italy. He did not protest returning to Manhattan.

Back in New York with Gwyn, however, he found that his restlessness persisted. Wasn't there *any* place he could really relax? He wondered. Time and again he thought of California. Late in '44 he made three important announcements in letters to Dook — a son, Thom, had been born to Gwyn in New York on August 4, 1944; in just six weeks there he had written *Cannery Row*; and he and Gwyn were preparing to move back to California. "I've a wonderful sense of going home," he said. " . . . I'd like to settle there if I can. Gwyn and baby are flying out and I am driving . . . with household goods. I'll make it in six to eight days with luck."

Reaching Monterey, he bought the old Spanish house he had wanted since boyhood — the historic Casa de Soto at 460 Pierce Street, sadly in need of renovation. In the autumn of '44 he learned that an old friend was in town — Lloyd Shebley! Lloyd had just arrived on a shrimp boat which he had rented in San Francisco to sail down the coast "for a little fishing." He had anchored in Monterey, expecting to stay only a few days, and had rented a cheap room in a fleatrap hotel on the waterfront, where John found him. It was an exciting reunion, but the most excited of all was Lloyd's Mexican landlady, long a Steinbeck fan. "Jus' theenk," she kept repeating, "a famous man like Senor Steinbeck come to my hotel! Jus' theenk!" She moved Lloyd into a better room. No extra rent.

While Lloyd was in town, he pitched in to help John fix up his new house, all the while reminiscing about old days at Lake Tahoe. When it was time for Lloyd to leave on the shrimp boat, he and John said their goodbyes. They never saw one another again.

While in Monterey, John did his writing in an upstairs room of the Monterey County Trust and Savings Bank, a room he took when refused space in the "Professional" Building. The manager of the building was apparently suspicious of anyone so unstable as to write for a living and seemed not to recognize the Steinbeck name. Too bad he couldn't have talked with a certain Mexican woman who ran a fleatrap hotel in one of the less fashionable parts of town. During his Peninsula sojourn, John also spent much time with Ed Ricketts in the lab, was shocked to find that Ratzi (Tiny) Colletto of the old *Western Flyer* crew was dying, and was saddened to observe the aging process subtly at work on other old friends. Refreshing interludes came, however, when he laughed and talked ancient Middle English with his sister, Mary, now in Carmel.

His latest book, *Cannery Row* (published in December of 1944, but dated 1945), quickly became a topic of discussion and people would buttonhole him on the streets of Monterey to speak of it, but for the most part he was not happy. An ironic refrain must have come to mind — "I've a wonderful sense of going home. . . . I'd like to settle there if I can."

At one point he even toyed with the idea of buying land in the Corral de Tierra, property within sight of the age-old sandstone castles of his boyhood — the very castles his imaginative young mind had filled with Galahads and Lancelots.

"At the head of the canyon there stands a tremendous stone castle, buttressed and towered like those strongholds the Crusaders put up in the path of their conquests. Only a close visit to the castle shows it to be a strange accident of time and water erosion working on the soft, stratified sandstone. In the distance the ruined battlements, the gates, the towers, even the arrow slits, require little imagination." — "The Murder" from *The Long Valley.*

However, he was discouraged by the asking price for the land he wanted, and sadly abandoned his sentimental notion — just as he gradually abandoned sentimental feelings about the Monterey Peninsula as a whole. Old friends and old haunts seemed changed. Plainly he had outgrown the place.

In 1945, the Steinbecks vacated their new home — at least for a time — and finally sold it a year later. By early February of 1945, John had finished a novelette whose working title was "The Pearl of LaPaz." It would appear ten months later in the December issue of *Woman's Home Companion* as "The Pearl of the World." Meanwhile, in Cuernavaca, Mexico, he helped director Emilio Fernandez film the story, which had now become simply *The Pearl*, a title it kept when published in book form in December 1947 and simultaneously released as a movie.

California, Mexico, New York — John's address shifted frequently during this period. In New York on June 12, 1946, a second, and last, child was born, John IV, nicknamed "Catbird." That same summer,

Steinbeck was writing *The Wayward Bus*, a story that had been fermenting for a long time. Its conception, in fact, may have gone as far back as 1940 when he had made the trip to Mexico City in the old bakery truck with panel body — a journey that would have given plenty of time for musing. As originally planned, the story was set in Mexico. By July of 1945, the theme had crystallized sufficiently to rough out the book's plot and structure. Again, his familiarity with ancient cars stood him in good stead, for a battered old bus served as his story device for bringing a motley group of passengers together for a few hours. The book was published early in 1947.

On a day in early May, 1948, John received a phone call in New York from Ritchie Lovejoy out in California. Ritchie's message left him thunderstruck, for he learned of Doc Ricketts' critical injuries in a train-car crash — the accident so graphically described by Steinbeck in "About Ed Ricketts" in *The Log From the Sea of Cortez*. Within hours, Steinbeck was on a plane flying west to be near his friend. The seriousness of Ricketts' condition, as he wavered between life and death, shocked him so greatly that a doctor found it necessary to give John a sedative and put him to bed. It was a crushing blow when Ed Ricketts died on May 11.

Another shock was in store. His marriage to Gwyn was falling apart, which did not surprise their friends, for they had long noted a growing coolness between them. Only a short time after the Ricketts tragedy, which hung over him inescapably, he saw that divorce was inevitable and in late August of 1948 signed an agreement settling property matters and all rights "with reference to the future custody, care, support, maintenance and education" of the two children. In October Gwyndolyn C. Steinbeck was granted her freedom in a Reno courtroom on the routine grounds of "extreme cruelty of a mental nature." The marriage had lasted five years.

Seized by a terrible depression as a result of unhappy events, Steinbeck sought relief in the only way he knew — by writing. He ploughed into it. Beginning in the fall of 1948, he began writing the script for *Viva Zapata!*, which was released by Twentieth Century-Fox in 1952, and he turned out two short stories, "The Miracle of Tapayac" (*Collier's*, December 25, 1948) and "His Father" (*Reader's Digest*, September 1949). But for once hard work proved no palliative. Nor did his old familiar surroundings, for in the spring of 1949 he was living again in the tiny Pacific Grove cottage where Dook paid a visit. Memories of Gwyn, the caller found, were plaguing him. "She took every goddamn thing I had," John said bitterly — a statement he amplified during the evening when he added, "By a curious trick she got all of my books — and certainly not because she wanted to read." In a letter fifteen years later John repeated himself almost verbatim.

Life moved gloomily along until a chance introduction profoundly affected his whole future. He met Elaine Scott.

Their meeting took place on Memorial Day, 1949, at Pebble Beach, where Elaine, wife of actor Zachary Scott, was on a brief vacation with actress Ann Sothern, who was acquainted with John. A handsome brunette of about thirty-four, of medium height, with a classical profile and flashing hazel eyes, Elaine spoke in a deep-throated voice that John found intriguing. She loved books and the stage and discussed them with concern and understanding. She was a native of Texas, a graduate of the University of Texas, and had already made her mark in the precarious profession of stage management, becoming the second woman stage manager on Broadway. They found they had mutual friends in New York.

Whatever chemical reaction was at work between the two, it deeply affected both of them. On the day they met, they sat talking for six solid hours. And didn't know where the time went.

On that complete and unexpected turnaround, Steinbeck's California life came to a close — and a full life it had been. Yet wasn't it only yesterday that he was a boy in a small town telling ghost stories on the front porch? And yesterday, when nine, that he fell under the spell of Malory's *Morte d'Arthur*? And yesterday, too, that he entered Stanford to become a writer? And now Elaine. . . .

Indeed the western experiences were a volume in themselves, an adventure story filled with hopes and disappointments, successes and bitterness — but it was one book that John never wrote.

He had been too busy living it.

EPILOGUE

IT was only a matter of time before Elaine obtained a divorce from Zachary Scott, and on December 28, 1950, a year and a half after their first meeting, John and Elaine were married in New York. Once again, he was eager to try married life in this big city of his boyhood choice. And this time he *knew* it would work. He felt it in his bones.

Although he was in familiar surroundings, it was the beginning of an entirely new mode of life for John. He became a debonair man about town, wore smartly tailored clothes and sometimes an opera cape with a red lining, swung a walking stick, and lived in a brownstone house, later moving into an elegant apartment on the thirty-fourth floor of a nearby highrise. Loving gadgetry, at times he even carried, but didn't use, a monocle. Only at home did he revert to the informality of old clothes — moccasins, sweat shirt, and comfortable khaki pants. Although he never forgot old aquaintances, numbered among his new friends were presidents and other men of state, artists, writers, and stage people, the famous and the unknown. When not in their Manhattan home, the Steinbecks were usually at their country retreat in Sag Harbor, Long Island, or traveling. They made fifteen trips abroad, their journeys taking them all over the world.

During these years he produced five novels, two books of nonfiction, and a musical comedy, together with newspaper and magazine articles. He engaged, also, in speech writing for Lyndon Johnson, and did some work for the United Nations as a result of his close friendship with Adlai Stevenson, then the UN Ambassador. The climax to his years as a writer came on December 10, 1962, in Stockholm, Sweden, when he received the Nobel Prize for Literature. Although this coveted recognition had been triggered by *The Winter of Our Discontent* and influenced by *Travels with Charley*, taken into consideration were the humor, social perception, sympathy for the oppressed, and wide appeal of his great body of work. He was only the sixth American to win the prestigious award, the others having been Sinclair Lewis, Pearl Buck, Eugene O'Neill, William Faulkner and Ernest Hemingway. His books had been translated into sixty languages.

Late in 1968 John was hospitalized with a serious heart condition, but begged to be taken to his New York apartment on East 72nd Street. The doctor consented. Those last weeks in his New York home were filled with nostalgia but outward lightheartedness. And although discordant notes must have been struck at times during their eighteen-year marriage, any differences would be hard now to imagine. While John spent much of his time in bed, beside which stood an oxygen tank regulated by Elaine, he also walked around in his dressing robe, stood briefly at their high windows, and watched TV, or read. There were many crises brought on by breathing problems, day and night. Regularly, Elaine checked his blood pressure and temperature, kept medical charts, and saw that he got the prescribed medications on schedule.

Lying in bed, John never mentioned the two symbolic angels hovering over him — two life-size papier-mâché figures supported above the bed by invisible bracing, decorative creations he had brought from Spain. But did they remind him of the line he had written about his early pneumonia? — "I went down and down until the wing tips of the angels brushed my eyes."

Sometimes he asked Elaine to read to him. And sometimes at night from a window they looked upon the city's million miles of neon, glowing far below.

At five-thirty on the afternoon of December 20, 1968, he died in bed, peacefully. More fortunate than most men, many of the dreams of his life had been realized. One in particular, always of fascination to him, had been almost realized — he had written a substantial portion of the Arthurian legend, only a little of it remaining unfinished. (His sister Mary had died in Carmel three years earlier, a loss that in some ways had brought him mystically closer to her and tightened his resolve to finish the book.)

Simple funeral rites were held at nearby St. James Episcopal Church. On Christmas Eve, Elaine and John's son, Thom, on leave from Vietnam, took John's ashes to the Monterey peninsula, where a private family memorial was held on Point Lobos, on a cliff overlooking Whaler's Bay — a spot that had been especially dear to John and his sister Mary. The place was heartbreakingly beautiful, with gulls soaring and a sea otter playing on the swells below.

Now John's ashes are buried beside his ancestors in the oak-shaded Salinas Garden of Memories. It is a quiet cemetery. Fremont's Peak rises in the east, and to the west, not far away, are the weathered sandstone castles of Corral de Tierra, surely still peopled with the gallant knights of old.

INDEX